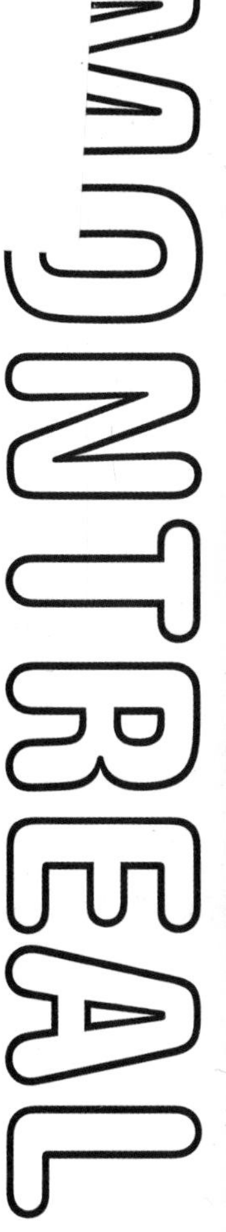

WEEKEND**escape**

Discover Montreal

Even though French is its official language, Montreal is nothing like a French city. Don't expect to find French attitudes or behavior, for Montreal is well and truly North American, with all the exuberance, hyperactivity and multicultural vitality this entails. This heritage can also be traced in the emphasis the city places not on the face it presents to the world, but on the atmosphere it exudes.

As in most of the large cities of this continent, architectural harmony is not the prime consideration. It's the aura of a town which embodies its beauty, and that's what gives Montreal its grace and grandeur. You only have to walk along Rue Sainte-Catherine (one of the key arteries of the city) to realize it. Neither handsome nor ugly, this street is bewildering, disconcerting and indescribable, yet it feels good to be there. Other areas strike you with the variety of their buildings or their ebullient atmosphere. The old town, for example, affectionately nicknamed "le Vieux" (the Old Man), has so distinct a character that it almost seems like a separate village. The subdued colors, the silence, the narrowness of the cobbled streets, the passing *calèches* and the nearness of the river draw us into another era, flecked with European traces. Away from the exuberance of the downtown area, you can easily fancy that time has stopped still as you go strolling on the promenade of the Vieux-Port (Old Port) or wander into the many art galleries that line rue Saint-Paul. In a completely different style, the streets of Plateau Mont-Royal form another distinct "village," utterly different from "le Vieux," but no less intrinsic to the city. Here, color is abundant, the little houses gleaming with yellow, pink, green and blue bricks. The semidetached houses of two or three stories proudly display outside stairways of bold and elegant designs worthy to be called works of art. This is a

residential district, where life is pleasant both indoors and out: a little corner of countryside where it's easy to forget you are in the heart of the city. But Montreal wouldn't be so attractive without its multicultural side. Its history has obviously encouraged the bilingualism of its citizens and the fruitful mingling of the two cultures, French and Anglo-Saxon; but it's more than that. Montreal is traditionally a landing point, welcoming immigrants in search of a place to live and express themselves freely. Thus many areas have formed themselves into micro-villages, according to the various ethnic communities that go to make up the city's rich tapestry of peoples. What could be more agreeable than to sip a cappuccino in Little Italy, buy a *pasteis de nata* at the Portuguese bakery on rue Duluth, to take one's pick of the exotic fruits in the Chinese quarter, or drop into Schwartz's and sample the delicious smoked meat that has become a symbol of Montreal? This pervasive multiculturalism, emblem of the city's broad-mindedness, makes room for everyone and explains why you always feel good in Montreal: an unconventional place, with no hang-ups, where imagination and creativity manifest themselves on the corner of every street. So, even though you might sometimes feel perplexed by the fragmented or hybrid architecture, a moment of discomfiture is well worth enduring for the warmth and humanity that the buildings emanate. Isn't this, after all, what matters: to enjoy a feeling of liberty and well-being, to climb to the top of Mont-Royal (affectionately referred to as "the Mountain" by Montrealers), fill your lungs with fresh air and admire the immense panorama that spreads out before you?

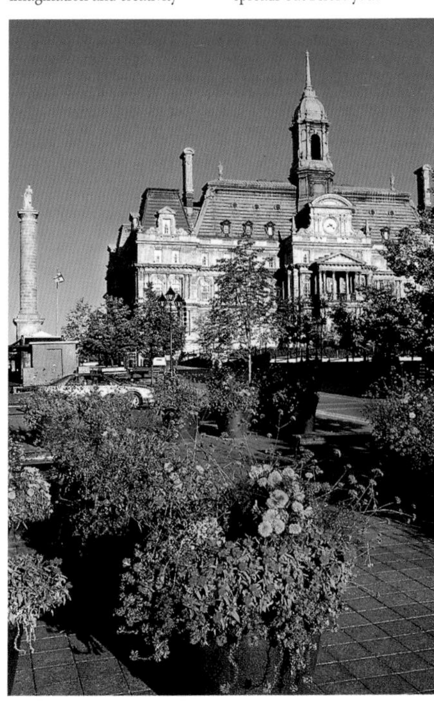

Practicalities

Climate

It's important to bear in mind what season it will be when you are planning your trip to Montreal. Dramatic temperature extremes orchestrate the town's rhythm and that of its inhabitants (see p. 16). In winter the cold predominates. As soon as October arrives the weather freshens and the first frosts are not far away. Icy temperatures encroach gradually as December advances, and the city is plunged into a period of intense cold (though with sunny skies), punctuated by snowstorms, until March or April. During this time, the thermometer dips to between -5° and -15°C without allowing for the wind-chill factor, which can make the temperatures plummet even further. April is changeable and unpredictable; only in May does a steady stream of fine days arrive. Then till the end of September the weather is sunny and pleasant, though July and August can be very warm (up to 30°C) and humid.

For detailed weather forecasts:

Meteorological Service of Canada
☎ (514) 283 3010
www.meteo.ec.gc.ca

Know before you go

Canadian Embassies

US (Los Angeles):
550, South Hope Street, 9th Floor, Los Angeles CA90071-2627
☎ (213) 346 2700
www.losangeles.gc.ca

UK:
Macdonald House, 1, Grosvenor Square, London W1X 0AB
☎ (020) 7258 6600
www.dfait-maeci.gc.ca/london

Australia:
Commonwealth Avenue, Canberra, ACT 2600
☎ (02) 6270 4000
www.dfait-maeci.gc.ca/australia

Ireland:
66, St. Stephen's Green, Dublin 2
☎ 01 417 4100
www.canadaeuropa.gc.ca/ireland

New Zealand:
PO Box 12049, Thorndon, Wellington
☎ (04) 473 9577
www.dfait-maeci.gc.ca/newzealand

South Africa:
1103, Arcadia Street, Hatfield, Pretoria 0028
☎ (012) 422 3000
www.consulfrance-jhb.org

Tourisme Montréal
www.tourisme-montreal.org
(Website of the Montreal tourist office, providing a wealth of information to help you make the most of your trip.)

How do I get there?

US airlines

The major US airlines offer regular flights between the US and Montreal.

American Airlines
☎ (800) 433 7300
www.aa.com

Delta
☎ (800) 221 1212
www.delta.com

Northwest
☎ (800) 447 4747
www.nwa.com

US Airways
☎ (800) 428 4322
www.usairways.com

Visitors from outside North America may find it worthwhile investigating connections via busy US–Canada routes. There are many special offers, but these require you to fly at specified times or dates.

Air Canada

☎ (888) 247 2262
www.aircanada.ca

Air Canada is the country's largest carrier and, in many instances, it has a monopoly. Regular flights arrive in Montreal from most major world cities. In addition to regularly scheduled services, its subsidiaries, Air Canada Tango (www.flytango.com; ☎ (800) 315 1390) and Air Canada Jazz (www.flyjazz.ca; ☎ (800) 315 1390) offer budget services.

Other Canadian airlines

Air Transat
☎ (877) 872 6728)
www.airtransat.com

Based in Montreal and best known for charter flights to Europe during the summer and services to vacation destinations in Florida and the Caribbean during the winter months.

Westjet
☎ (403) 250 5839
www.westjet.com

Founded in 1996, originally to provide a budget air service to western Canada, now also offers services between Montreal and many other Canadian and US cities. It is Canada's second-largest carrier, after Air Canada.

International airlines

International airlines with nonstop services to Montreal include the following:

British Airways
☎ (800) 247 9297
www.british-airways.com

Air France
☎ (800) 237 2747
www.airfrance.com

KLM
☎ (800) 447 4747
www.klm.com

Lufthansa
☎ (800) 563 5954
www.lufthansa.com

Qantas
☎ (800) 227 4500
www.qantas.com

From the airport to downtown

Taxis

Located about 12 miles from downtown Montreal, Montreal–Trudeau Airport is

ELECTRICITY

The electrical current in Canada is 110 volts. An adapter is needed for European electrical appliances.

easily accessible. The simplest way to go into town is by cab. The journey takes about 20 minutes for a fixed fare of $31 (plus tip).

Shuttle buses

There is also a shuttle-bus service that goes downtown, calling at certain big hotels (on demand). The buses operate between 7am and 1am, leaving every 30 minutes. In Montreal they stop at several places, including the main bus stations: Aerobus Station (777, rue de la Gauchetière Ouest, M° Bonaventure) and Central Station (505, bd de Maisonneuve Est, M° Berri-UQAM). Ask the driver whether there are any stops nearer to your hotel. Journey times vary according to the number of stops made, but the average time is about 45 minutes. You can buy your ticket from the driver or, for the return journey, from the bus station itself. Count on spending about $12 per adult for a one-way ticket and $21.75 round-trip. Children aged between five and 12 and persons over 65 pay a reduced fare. Infants up to the age of five travel for free.

Public transport

The last option is public transport. This is the least expensive but also the least convenient of the various choices. On leaving the airport you take bus no. 204 for Dorval Station. On arrival at the station, get on either bus no. 211, which will take you to Lionel Groulx subway station, or the suburban train for Lucien-L'Allier, also a downtown subway station (orange line). To pay, you must purchase a bus ticket ($2.50 each) for route 204. Be sure to make clear, when buying your ticket, if you want a transfer. If you then decide to take a second bus, the driver will have given you a transfer and you won't have to buy another ticket (don't forget to ask for another connection ticket if you are continuing via the subway). If you prefer to take the suburban train, you will have to pay 75 cents at Dorval Station for a train-bus-subway combination ticket.

STM
☎ (514) 288 6287
www.stm.info
For information about bus schedules.
ATM ☎ (514) 287 8726
www.amt.qc.ca
For information about train schedules.
Aérobus
☎ (514) 931 9002 or 1 (888) 872 5525
www.autobus.qc.ca
Aéroport Pierre-Elliott-Trudeau
☎ (514) 394 7377
www.admtl.com

Formalities

American citizens must show proof of citizenship when entering Canada. At the present time a passport is not essential, though it is the best and easiest way to prove your citizenship. Otherwise any documentation with photo ID can be used, such as a certificate of naturalization.
EU and Australian citizens do not need a visa for tourist visits of less than three months. You do, however, need a valid passport (with an expiry date of not less

than six months after your planned return).

Customs

Everyone over the age of 16 has the right to import, duty-free, 200 cigarettes, 50 cigars or 14 ounces of manufactured tobacco. Only those over 18 years of age can import alcohol: more precisely, 1.5 liters of alcohol (including wine) or 8 liters of beer. Generally speaking, don't bring perishable goods, since Canadian law is particularly strict about such items. For any further information, contact the Canadian embassy (see p. 4).

Health

No vaccinations are required. If you are taking any special medication, make sure to take enough with you, for it may not be readily available once you get there. Medical expenses, particularly hospital bills, are significantly higher than in Europe. You may wish to buy travel insurance before your departure; in which case, consult your bank, since most bank cards offer such policies.

Currency

Legal currency is the Canadian dollar; there are 100 cents to the dollar. Bills of 5, 10, 20, 50, 100 and 1,000 dollars, and coins of 5, 10 and 25 cents and 1 and 2 dollars, are in circulation. Be careful not to confuse the Canadian with the American dollar: they do not have the same value. Make sure you have some cash with you on arrival, to pay for your cab or bus ticket into town. The exchange rates vary from day to day, but, as an indication only, they were as follows at the time of printing:
US$1 = $1.18 CDN and
£1 = $2.00 CDN;
or, roughly speaking, $12 CDN is the equivalent of US$10. All prices in this book are in Canadian dollars. For further details on foreign exchange offices, see p. 35.

Your budget

The variable exchange rate means you can only budget at the time of departure. Your daily expenditure will also depend on which category of hotel you have chosen, but, aside from the cost of your accommodation, a minimum of $80 will allow you to spend an agreeable day (not counting shopping expenses, naturally).

Time difference

Montreal and most of the province of Quebec observes Eastern Standard Time (EST), the same as New York or Miami. This is five hours ahead of Co-ordinated Universal Time (formerly known as GMT). So noon in Montreal will be 5pm in London.

PUBLIC HOLIDAYS

Banks, government offices and some private businesses are closed on the following holidays:

New Year's Day (January 1)
Good Friday
Easter Monday
Victoria Day, or National Patriots' Day (the Monday before May 25)
St John the Baptist's Day (June 24)
Canada Day (July 1)
Labour Day (1st Monday in September)
Thanksgiving Day (2nd Monday in October)
Christmas Day (December 25)

From "Ville-Marie" to "Montreal": the story of a city

Like all the great cities of North America, Montreal has grown up from the different immigrant communities settled there through the centuries. But it is one of those rare places that have been able to preserve the traditions and identity of each one.

The birth of Ville-Marie

On May 17, 1642 a French missionary colony of about 50 pioneers, led by Sieur (Lord) Paul Chomedey of Maisonneuve, founded Ville-Marie, with the purpose of converting the Native Americans to Catholicism. Although the evangelization of the local people made little headway, many religious communities were soon established on the isle, and by 1666 priests of the Sulpician order were the new masters. Six years later, the first streets of the town, rechristened Montreal in 1685, had appeared. The settlement became the focal point for fur trading and a substantial military base for sorties against the British colonies and their Iroquois allies. A fortified wall was subsequently constructed around the city, between 1717 and 1744. But despite this, and in consequence of the Seven Years' War that rampaged across Europe, France signed the Treaty of Paris in 1763, yielding its Canadian lands to Britain.

The British regime

From that date, the town underwent a change of character. French-speaking citizens were excluded from all major decision-making until 1774, while English-speaking entrepreneurs took control of all financial and commercial networks. Several small fur-trading companies merged, in 1779, to form the North West Company, which by 1804 held the monopoly of trade in Montreal, before merging in its turn, in 1821, with the Hudson's Bay Company, which is still in business today!

The demolition of the fortifications began in 1804; the city expanded adding more streets. Its population increased with a huge influx of immigrants from Britain and its territories, especially Ireland. Between 1815 and 1850, Montreal, with a majority by now of English-speakers, was regarded as the principal city of British North America.

Accelerating industrialization

At the end of the 19th century, Montreal was clearly dominated by the Anglo-Scottish bourgeoisie, as evidenced by the appearance on the streets of prestigious buildings in a Victorian style (see p. 14). The development of the town advanced rapidly, with the emergence of distinct middle-class, working-class and industrial areas, along with the thrusting upwards of

the first skyscrapers. The Lachine Canal was widened in 1840 (see p. 68); in 1881 the Canadian Pacific Railway was begun. These formidable engineering projects, requiring a huge workforce for their realization, provoked a massive exodus of French Canadians from the countryside, soon reversing the linguistic balance of the city (see p. 12). From 1900 to 1950, Montreal grew, thanks to its rail and maritime transport network, into the main industrial complex in the country, as well as the chief financial center.

THE QUIET REVOLUTION

In the 1960s, Montreal, and Quebec province in general, underwent a radical change.
The Liberal Party won the elections, returning economic, political, financial and cultural power to the Francophone elite. Another major upset was the separation of church and state, ensuring the secularization of education, the civil service, health and social services. These measures gave rise to serious stresses, ending in the adoption of Law 101 (see p. 13). At the same time, the city was modernized with the construction of the subway system and the indoor city (see p. 28), as well as the erection of state-of-the-art skyscrapers. Spectacular events, such as the 1967 Exposition and the 1976 Olympic Games, contributed equally to the town's urban and economic development and confirmed Montreal's place among the great cities of the world.

A green metropolis

With more than 450,000 trees, over a third of which line its streets, Montreal surely deserves its reputation as a green city. It has needed considerable political will to preserve, develop and enhance the town's green spaces and public highways.

Major parks

An essential feature of the Montreal landscape, Parc du Mont-Royal, occupying the majestic "Montagne" ("Mountain) in the heart of the city, is indisputably the most renowned of Montreal's parks (see pp. 65 and 81). A surface area of 250 acres contains more than 150 species of birds and about 700 plant and tree varieties, mainly white ash, silver maple and red oak. Its sloping location offers marvelous viewpoints on the city. The 550 acre Parc Jean-Drapeau, spread across two islands, is an oasis of green set right in

the middle of the Saint Lawrence River. In addition to the numerous footpaths that thread through the park, the gardens and canals of the Floralies offer one of the most delightful walks in this island jewel. Less exuberant but just as pleasant, La Fontaine Park is a glorious haven of peace in the center of the Plateau (see p. 59).

Botanical Garden

Sequestered in the bosom of Maisonneuve Park, Montreal's Botanical Garden is among the finest and most extensive in the world. As well as its magnificent exhibition conservatories and its many thematic gardens (see pp. 70 and 80), it displays some lush vegetation. More than half its surface area is given over to the Arboretum, a veritable forest in the heart of the city, comprising 7,000 species of trees and shrubs split among 45 collections. Lovers of shady walks will take equal pleasure in the First Nations' Garden, the aim of which is to embody the harmony in which the Native American and Inuit peoples have always lived with the plant world. Three types of habitat are represented: conifer forests, broad-leaved forests and Nordic territory.

Gardens and green spaces

In addition to these large-scale natural attractions, Montreal boasts a multitude of small gardens and green areas scattered throughout its length and breadth. Among these is the splendid Governor's Garden, located at the back of the Château Ramezay (see p. 40). Comprising a kitchen garden, an orchard and an ornamental garden, it offers, together with the small park laid out alongside the Old Port, one of the finest little spots of greenery in Old Montreal. The Outremont area is also very rich in green spaces (see pp. 62-63). With its numerous parks, its exceptionally leafy streets and its proximity to the imposing garden of Mont-Royal Cemetery (see p. 65), it offers some magnificent walks. For those who prefer something a little more intellectual, the Architecture Garden in the Canadian Centre of Architecture (CCA) recalls the city's history: a perfect balance between nature and culture (see p. 15).

A city in flower

From May onwards, Montreal is dressed in its loveliest garments. The city has numerous greenhouses where more than 1.2 million flowering plants are nurtured. Of these, 500,000 are given free to Montrealers, to embellish their balconies and terraces! You have to stroll down the streets of Plateau Mont-Royal to enjoy the shimmering scene to the full. In addition, the landscape gardeners seem to want to make the city blossom, resulting in some amazing floral sculptures adorning the sidewalks. The fountain located in the town-hall square is a perfect example. And so, until winter clamps down once more, Montreal arrays herself in the colors and scents of an extended festival.

COMMUNITY GARDENS

For $10 a year, Montrealers can rent a small garden patch of 3 by 6 yards. To meet aesthetic standards, each gardener must devote 75 percent of this plot to vegetables and 25 percent to flowers, herbs or fruits. There are 94 community gardens and 8,400 individual allotments spread throughout the isle of Montreal. Citizens take this pastime so seriously that every year the city organizes a competition for the "best gardener of Montreal."

Bilingual, cosmopolitan and multicultural

The flag of Montreal, displaying the French lily, the English rose, the Scottish thistle and the Irish shamrock, is an important symbol, for it is this cultural mixture that creates the soul of the city and gives it its richness. Bilingual and cosmopolitan, Montreal is a town of many faces, whose ethnic patchwork constitutes its greatness and its individuality.

The French

Even though French is still the official language of Quebec, it hasn't always been easy for French-speaking Quebecers – or Québécois – to impose their language. With the inauguration of British rule in 1763 and the years of transition that followed, French Canadians became a minority and the practice of their language was increasingly overshadowed. It was only at the end of the 19th century, as the result of a massive rural exodus and several waves of migrants, that the city's linguistic pendulum began to swing the other way. Today Francophones constitute more than 67 percent of inhabitants of the Montreal conurbation. In Montreal itself, although no clear limits have been defined, they continue to form a majority east of Boulevard Saint-Laurent, with the Latin Quarter as their cultural stronghold (see p. 56).

The Anglophones

A minority in Quebec, but the majority in Canada as a whole, the Anglophones of Montreal nurse ambiguous feelings about where they belong, and many will tell you that they feel themselves to be more Canadian than Québécois. Yet Montreal would lose its identity if it was stripped of its English-speaking community. Clustered essentially in the west of the city, the Anglophones are ensconced in classy areas such as Westmount (see p. 66) or the Golden Square Mile (see p. 50). It was in this quarter in the course of the 19th century that rich English and Scottish businessmen established themselves and made an important contribution to

the economic growth of the city. Nowadays, despite the political steps taken to protect and impose the French language, the Anglophones remain in Montreal without surrendering anything of their language or identity.

Two cultures?

It is this cultural mix which lends Montreal its uniqueness and, it must be admitted, certain advantages: 53 percent of the population is completely bilingual. But this cohabitation of two languages has given rise

to intermittent tension. Anglophones and Francophones, both construing themselves to be in the minority, live haunted by the same fear: disappearance. And yet the city fosters two French and two English universities, offers four public television channels (two in English, two in French) as well as any number of newspapers and magazines in both languages. Isn't this proof positive that the mutual respect between the two coexisting groups forms an integral part of the Montreal identity?

The ethnic communities

The cultural mosaic does not end here, for there are many other smaller ethnic groupings to be taken into account. The most numerous is the Italian community, but there are also other languages spoken in the home. These are, in decreasing order of the number of users: Arabic, Spanish, various Creole languages, Chinese, Greek, Portuguese and Vietnamese, as well as the important community of Orthodox Jews. Thus each group contributes to the diversity and effervescence of the urban landscape: Little Italy abounds in Mediterranean offerings (see p. 60), the Chinese quarter is replete with exotic color (see p. 53), the cafés and restaurants of the Portuguese enliven the sidewalks in the Plateau area. This multinational tableau is one of the city's most valuable treasures.

LAW 101

In 1969, a protest by nationalists alarmed by the Anglicization of new immigrants made itself heard. On August 6, 1977, the Parti québécois (Quebecers' Party) enacted Law 101, establishing French as the language of the workplace, commerce and business. The law required new immigrants with parents who had not taken courses in English in Canada to be enrolled in French-speaking schools. This 'Quebec charter', still in force, constituted unprecedented linguistic enforcement.

The city reflected in its architecture

Some visitors may feel bewildered when faced with the architectural anarchy that holds sway in Montreal. Others, on the contrary, will fall under the peculiar spell of the buildings, discerning the history and soul of the city through its miscellany of styles. Montreal comprises an urban landscape that is rich and eclectic, a true reflection of the people that have built it and the various cultures that animate it.

The old town

Declared a historic district in 1964 by the government of Quebec, this small area of less than half a square mile, its perimeter determined by the layout of the old fortified town, encloses a unique architectural heritage. Its stone houses and cobbled streets give it the atmosphere of a village. The oldest residential building – the Old Seminary at 130, rue Notre-Dame Ouest – dates back to 1684. Most of the buildings, however, date from the 19th century, and, although different styles sit side-by-side, Old Montreal evinces a certain harmony, thanks to the opaqueness of the dwellings, the lack of adornment and greenery, and the narrowness of the streets. The buildings constructed between 1800 and 1850 express a sober neoclassicism, from their British origin. The years 1850 to 1880 gave birth to buildings in a Victorian style that was weightier and more imposing. They now rose to four stories and devoted more space to windows. The buildings located between 451 and 457 on Rue Saint-Pierre are good examples of these.

Skyscrapers and modernism

If Old Montreal has preserved an air of exemplary sobriety, the business center exudes the upward-thrusting modernism and exuberance characteristic of North America. It was at the beginning of the 1960s that the first contemporary skyscrapers appeared, with the opening of Place Ville-Marie in 1962 (see pp. 29 and 46). Since then, numerous ultramodern glass towers have taken root in the urban landscape, such as the IBM-Marathon Tower (1250, bd René-Lévesque Ouest), the BNP Tower (1981, av McGill College) and the famous 1000 De la Gauchetière Tower, a skyscraper of 51 floors, completed in 1992 and attaining the maximum height allowed by the city: 764ft, the same height as the summit of Mont-Royal Park. Hemmed in between the downtown area and Old Montreal, the recently developed international quarter has produced modern structures of originality and audacity, such as the Caisse de Dépôts et de Placements (Bank of Deposits and Investments), the Montreal World Trade Center and the newly completed Palais de Congrès (Convention Center; see p. 45), with its enormous, eye-catching façade of colored glass.

Kaleidoscopic setting

Outside of its "old town" and its "modern town," Montreal shows a new face with every street. Each quarter shows off its individuality: Westmount with its sumptuous houses in

the English style (see p. 66), the Chinese quarter with its gateways and pagodas (see p. 53), and Plateau Mont-Royal, whose famous three-story houses with outside stairways add so much to the architectural character of the city (see pp. 58 and 82). The Anglo-Saxon heritage is also clearly discernible, notably in the little houses of brick or colored stone with elevated front doors and idiomatic external adornments (turrets, cornices, pediments, gables and so forth): Place Saint-Louis offers a superb example (see p. 57). The religious patrimony also contributes to the beauty and variety of the urban scene. Although many buildings have been demolished, one can still find more than five hundred churches, temples and mosques spread across the whole island. Among the most impressive, the Basilique Notre Dame (see pp. 44 and 85) and the Oratoire Saint-Joseph (see pp. 65 and 76) are well worth a visit.

CANADIAN CENTER FOR ARCHITECTURE (CCA)

Inaugurated in 1989, the CCA is both a museum (mounting temporary exhibitions) and a center of architectural research. The library contains one of the largest collections of publications and documents on architectural design in the world. The building encloses the Shaughnessy House, built in 1874, an authentic relic of the bourgeois dwellings that once occupied the area.

1920, rue Bayle
☎ (514) 939 7026
www.cca.qc.ca
Wed.-Sun. 10am-5pm (until 9pm Thu.).

The seasonal cycle

Montreal has warm, humid summers and glacial winters whose duration and intensity remind one that the Great North is not far away. Sandwiched between these two extremes, autumn and spring are just short interludes before the arrival of the next season.

Spring

After the long winter months, spring is welcomed like a gift from heaven. Even if they have to wait until May for a rise in temperature, everybody knows that winter is on its last legs.

The arrival of this season is celebrated with the "temps des sucres" (Maple Sugar Time; see p. 18). As soon as they can, Montrealers make a beeline for the sugar shacks to gorge themselves on delicacies.

During this time, the streets of the city remain buried in slush – old snow, black and muddy, which, as it begins to melt, reveals something of the degradation to the road surface caused by the ferocity of winter. When May comes, nature is reborn, warmth makes itself at home once more and the citizens' spirits begin to soar. Summer at last!

Summer

As if to make up for the imprisonment enforced by the harshness of winter, in summer everyone lives outdoors. Light clothing is worn, people greet each other and get together on café terraces or in one of the many city parks, to share enjoyable moments of conviviality and relaxation. Montreal has become a green and flower-filled city (see p. 10) and it's a real pleasure to survey the streets of the Plateau or to

stroll on the islands of Parc Jean-Drapeau. The city makes every effort to take advantage of this season, with a plethora of festivals and open-air events (see p. 20). Montrealers love to make merry, and crowds fill the streets until late in the evening (especially during the jazz festival).
The months of July and August can be stifling and humid, but what does that matter: this weather will soon be over, so why grumble? September is very pleasant and, even though it's back to work for most people, the days are full of enchantment.

Autumn

Does this season really exist? It is not unusual for temperatures to remain summery until October, the so-called Indian summer. Then, virtually from one day to the next, the first cool drafts, accompanied by night frosts, begin to bite. Winter is on the doorstep. September is the time to walk in the parks and forests and discover the marvelous scenery created by nature. Trees are steeped in magnificent shades of yellow, red and orange: a tableau emblematic of North America. By the end of October, the leaves have fallen and it's time to batten down for the months ahead.

Winter

Adored and hated simultaneously, winter is the harshest season of the calendar. From November to March, cold lays hold of the city and continual snowstorms from December to March (even April) govern the lives of the inhabitants. The annual budget for clearing snow from 2,900 miles of road and 3,900 miles of sidewalk (across the whole island) comes to about $65 million. Snowplowing is more than just a way of life, it's a veritable industry that has to be cranked into gear.
But what typifies the Montreal winter above all else is the brilliant sunshine. The sky is blue, rays of sunlight shimmer on the snow and the air is invigorating. Despite the low temperatures (which can dip to -30°C), Montrealers seize every opportunity to take advantage of the delights of the outdoors. Skiing on Mont-Royal or ice-skating are universal pastimes in this season (see p. 22). And when the wind becomes too tempestuous, giving rise to the phenomenon of *poudrerie* (whereby a mass of snow is lifted up, forming a whirlwind), it is high time to seek refuge in the underground city, there to find warmth and rediscover the joys of shopping (see p. 28).

IT'S TIME TO MOVE!

If Montreal has a distinctive seasonal ritual, it could well be Moving Day. In order not to disrupt the scholarly rhythm of its children and give them enough time to get used to a new location before beginning their next school year, the government of Quebec has decided that the leases on all rented accommodation should begin on July 1. As a result, on that day, which is also a national holiday (Canada Day), 250,000 households move their location, adding a uniquely picturesque charm to the streets of Montreal!

The maple leaf: story of an emblem

If the maple leaf has become the emblem on the Canadian flag, it's not by mere chance. Extracted from the sap of this majestic tree, maple syrup, the refining of which goes back many centuries, is integral to Quebec culture. Used every day in the kitchen, its production is not only an art. It has become a vital traditional festival, celebrating the arrival of spring and the rebirth of nature.

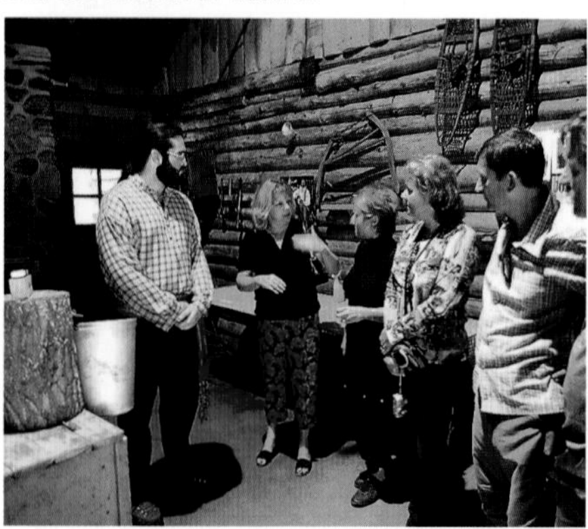

A short history

The silver maple, or red maple is a tree variety specific to North America and can reach a height of 130ft.
The Native Americans were the first to discover the edible properties of its sap, and it's thanks to their ingenuity that the early French colonists learned the techniques of collecting the sugary liquid. An authentic source of pure sugar, this quality beverage soon underwent the transformation of an industrial process.
Today 80 percent of global production of maple syrup takes place in Quebec.

Maple Sugar Time

Beginning in the months of March and April, "le temps des sucres" (Maple Sugar Time) is a important seasonal ritual. As well as announcing the preparation of numerous delicacies, it marks (at last!) the end of winter. To harvest the sap, the *acériculteur* (maple syrup producer) pierces the tree trunk and inserts a small metallic pipe from which is suspended a receptacle. Owing to the thaw, the sap, until now frozen through the winter, begins to liquefy and drip slowly into the container. Forty liters are needed to produce just one liter of syrup. It is in the traditional sugar shack that, once it has been collected, this sweetened water is brought to the boil and transformed into an incredibly aromatic syrup.

Let the feast begin

A celebration would be a poor affair without a feast. In consequence, "le temps des sucres" is synonymous with "le temps des festins" (Feasting Time). The sugar shacks become illustrious eating establishments, with their famous traditional menu of pea soup, *oreilles de crisse* ("Christ's ears," deep-fried crescents of pork skin), sausages, pies, maple-glazed ham, potatoes, omelettes, pork and beans, pancakes (with, of course, maple syrup), assorted fruit ketchup and sugared tarts: in short, a fairly copious meal that allows every food lover to "se sucrer le bec" (savor something sweet). And, to ensure that nobody is left unhappy, the sugar shack La Sucrerie de la Montagne is open all year through (see p. 74).

Syrup, butter, sugar or taffy?

Even though the reputation of maple syrup is well established, it is not the only product of the maple tree. Depending on the degree of boiling to which the sap is subjected, it can be made into syrup, butter, sugar or the irresistible maple taffy. Produced from a further cooking of the syrup, the taffy becomes a thick substance resembling honey. It is then deposited on snow and collected up by means of a short stick. This is the most coveted delicacy of the feast. As for maple butter, it's a simple spread with an enticing aroma.
Maple syrup itself comes in several varieties: extra clear, clear, medium or amber. But the differences in taste may be appreciated only by those with well-developed and experienced palates.

HAM GLAZED WITH MAPLE SYRUP

3.5 to 3.5lb boneless ham
2.5 fluid oz. maple syrup
tsp dry mustard
tbsp lemon juice

Preheat the oven to 160° F. Place the ham, fatty side up, on a shallow dish covered with large sheets of aluminum foil. Mark the meat with a criss-cross pattern and remove surplus fat. Blend the maple syrup, mustard and lemon juice. Smear this mixture onto the ham and seal it hermetically in the aluminum foil. Place in oven and allow to cook for 2 hours.

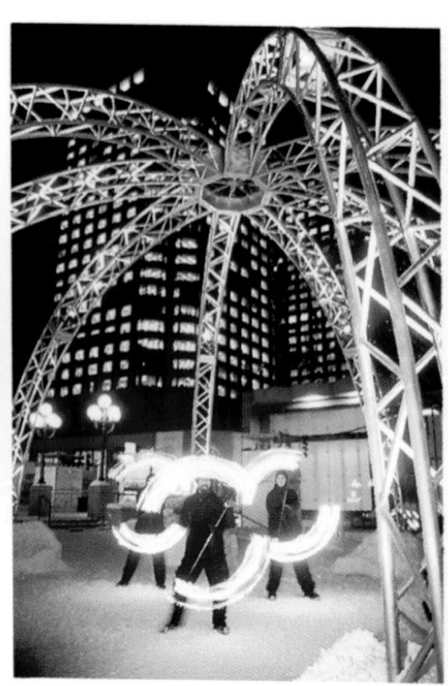

Festivals and celebrations

Justly considered a city of festivals, Montreal moves to the rhythm of its multiple events. Beyond their cultural and festive aspects, these happenings bear witness to an impressive feat of organization, requiring the deployment of a formidable infrastructure. Montrealers love festivities and are expert at creating them – the city responds to their efforts.

A city bubbling with excitement

With about 50 festivals of international renown, not to mention countless local events, Montreal is definitely one of the most festive cities in the world. Most of the big celebrations take place between May and October, many of them occurring in the open air. This can be put down in part to the desire of the inhabitants to take maximum advantage of the long, fine summer days, but it is also thanks to city policy, which allows festival organizers freedom to close off the streets. As a result, as well as the large-scale events, the streets are bristling with pavement stalls (see p. 101) and other festive and cultural gatherings, like the famous "Frénésies de la Main" ("Main" frenzies) which erupt every year between June and August along Boulevard Saint-Laurent, known as "Main" (see p. 54).

Some important festivals

February
Montreal Festival of Light
☎ (514) 288 9955
www.montrealenlumiere.com

May
Festival of Theater from the Americas
☎ (514) 871 2224
www.fta.qc.ca

June
Mutek (music, sound and new technologies)
☎ (514) 847 3536
www.mutek.ca
Formula 1 Grand Prix
☎ (514) 350 0000
www.grandprix.ca

June–July
Mondial SAQ (international fireworks competition)
☎ (514) 397 2000
www.lemondialsaq.com
Montreal International Jazz Festival
☎ (514) 871 1881
www.montrealjazzfest.com

July
Just for Laughs Festival
☎ (514) 845 3155
www.hahaha.com
African Nights Festival
☎ (514) 499 9239
www.festivalnuitsdafrique.com
FrancoFolies
☎ (514) 523 3378
www.francofolies.com

August
World Film Festival
☎ (514) 848-3883
www.ffm-montreal.org
Contact the tourist office for a full calendar of events (see p. 35).

Humor
No sooner has the last jazz-note died away than humor bursts onto the streets.
A few yards away from Place des Arts, around Rue Saint-Denis, new stages are set, this time to welcome the most talented contemporary humorists, for ten days of caustic comedy. More than 500 shows are staged indoors and about 1,600 outdoors, including theater performances as well as ludicrous antics to keep the children amused. This is the festival at its height.

Montreal in lights
Even though summer is the high season for festivals, winter also has its grand occasion with the Montreal Festival of Light.
For ten days in late February, the city is alive with concerts and various spectacles (some of them in the open air), featuring all-night dance, theater and acrobatics. Numerous culinary events are also programmed, and some formidable firework displays. Who said that winter was a miserable time of year?

JAZZ
The International Jazz Festival is indisputably the highlight of the summer. The Place des Arts and its environs are placed at the service of the audience, to accommodate the festival's ten outdoor stages. The program is impressive, with 40 or so concerts each day, two thirds of which are free. Even though jazz reigns supreme, with the current leading musicians in attendance, the festival also opens its arms to groups from other musical worlds, such as funk and world music. From noon through midnight, and often later, Montrealers live outdoors, while the city's arteries pulsate with *joie de vivre*.

Sport, a way of life

In North America, sport, taken up by children virtually from the cradle, is an integral part of daily life. It's a pastime highly prized and is considered as both a leisure activity and a way of keeping healthy. In Montreal, the natural world is on the doorstep, allowing open-air sports to be enjoyed throughout the year.

Cycling and summer sports

More than just a leisure activity, cycling is a serviceable means of transportation. It is thought that about 150,000 people take to their bicycles when the weather is fine. This isn't surprising, since on Montreal island there are more than 210 miles of bicycle tracks, linking up all the city's major parks. The Vieux-Port Promenade and the banks of the Lachine Canal, 9 miles in all, offer one of the pleasantest routes. The specially made paths are equally attractive to rollerbladers. The city's location is also ideal for water sports. Parc Jean-Drapeau is blessed with a beach of fine sand and a complex of outdoor swimming pools. The Olympic Basin on Île Notre Dame offers the chance to practice kayaking, sailboarding or pedal boating (also possible in the Vieux-Port). For some refreshing excitement, rafting down the Lachine Rapids is on offer.

Skiing and ice-skating

Is the winter icy and snowy? Better make the most of it, then. Bicycles are swapped for skis and skates, for several months of much enjoyed sliding about! And, as it happens, you won't have to go too far to enjoy your favorite sport. Among other blessings, the isle of Montreal proudly possesses 900 open-air skating rinks and about 425 miles of *pistes* (tracks) for cross-country skiing. Parc du Mont-Royal alone offers 12 miles of pistes of varying

difficulty. The city's other principal parks, such as La Fontaine or Maisonneuve, are equally devoted to sport at this time. As for ice rinks, the most important is undoubtedly the one at Bonsecours Basin, located near quai de l'Horloge in the Vieux-Port. Here the evenings are often musical and the atmosphere frenetic. Those who prefer a more intimate ambience go to the lakes in the parks, such as Lac des Castors (Beaver Lake) in Mont-Royal or other small skating rinks set up by the city just for the occasion. In

short, Montrealers have the chance to practice whatever winter sport they want, as soon as they leave the office; and they make good use of this opportunity. Besides, the downtown indoor ice-rink is open all year round and ever popular with Montreal's residents and guests.

Hockey

More than just a sport, ice hockey is a passion, a national symbol that provokes heated discussion, even about where it came from! Thanks to the city's numerous rinks, children are able to practice hockey throughout the year, helping the sport maintain its perennial popularity. The National Hockey League was founded in 1917, and comprises at present 30 clubs spread across the whole of North America. Montreal's team, the Canadians, has enjoyed its moments of glory, which the city's inhabitants still discuss with glowing pride. Players like Maurice "the Rocket" Richard have become national legends. On evenings when a game is taking place the streets near the stadium become very crowded. Montrealers who don't have tickets for the game crowd into sport-oriented bars such as Champs (3956, bd Saint-Laurent) or Upper Deck (1433, rue Crescent). It's all part of the tradition.

SOME EVENTS ON THE SPORTING CALENDAR

June
Canadian Formula 1 Grand Prix (Gilles-Villeneuve circuit)

August
Canadian Tennis Masters (men's tournament); Rogers AT&T Cup (women's tournament)

May
Féria de vélo (Montreal Bike Fest)

October through June
NHL ice hockey championships

Flavors of Quebec

Montreal's cuisine is like its citizens: multicultural. In addition, with its more than 5,000 restaurants, Montreal has something for every taste. The inhabitants certainly have a sweet tooth, and like bons vivants everywhere, they don't trouble to hide their love of good food. Even though some local dishes may lack a certain refinement, the variety and quality of Quebec recipes will titillate your taste buds.

Traditional specialties

You will soon discover that traditional Quebec dishes are not renowned for their lightness! Rich and generously proportioned, they helped the early settlers to get through the harsh winters. Even their names evoke their substantial nature: *tourtière* (meat pie), Chinese pâté (shepherd's pie garnished with corn), *cretons* (an assortment of *rillettes*, or meat pâtés), *oreilles de crisse* ("Christ's ears," strips of fried rind), beans in bacon, pea soup or, better still, *poutine* (potatoes covered with melted cheese curds and with brown gravy whose recipe is a well-kept secret). You can sample these in restaurants such as La Sucrerie de la Montagne (see p. 74), Le Cabaret du Roy (see p. 41) or La Binerie (see p. 93). For true epicures, Au Pied au Cochon offers a delicious *poutine au foie gra* (see p. 58).

Regional produce

Don't believe, though, that th food on your plate will show a lack of refinement. You'll also be surprised by the tastiness of the local fruit and vegetables. To sample these delights of th

alate all you need do is vander through Jean-Talon Market and browse freely among the great variety of roducts (see p. 60). At the same time you can ry some of the local pecialties, such as *crosses le fougères* (fern crosiers), *êtes de violon* ("fiddleheads," lelicious as salad or to add aroma to a sauce), ranberries (their slightly acid flavor adds marvelous iquancy to the famous Christmas turkey) or lueberries (especially the arge ones used in pastry lishes). As for the corn, nown as "Indian wheat," t is incredibly soft and sweet.

Bagels and smoked meat

Introduced into Montreal at he start of the 20th century, thanks to Jewish immigration from eastern Europe, these two specialties are among the most popular in the city. Made by hand, the bagels are blanched in boiling water to which a soupcon of honey has been added, before being baked in a wood stove. They can be "natural" or "flavored," usually with sesame or poppy seeds (try them in Fairmount Bagel, p. 63, or St-Viateur Bagel, p. 119). Better not tell them you prefer the American ones, or a potential friendship will be ruined! Montrealers also set great store by their smoked meat. It can be eaten on its own or in sandwiches, and, if the lunchtime line outside Schwartz's is anything to go by, it has become a national institution (see p. 55).

Beer

Although a recent survey indicates that wine has taken the lead, Montrealers have long been lovers of beer. Not content with merely drinking it, they also make it. The two large Quebec breweries, Molson's and Labatt's, have been joined by many small-scale breweries known as microbreweries (see p. 134). They create beers of subtly distinct flavors on the premises. The most popular are bottled under the labels of Maudite, Blanche de Chambly, Cap Tourmente, Fin du Monde, Saint-Ambroise and Berlue. When it's time for *l'appero* (the celebrated "happy hour"), before a hockey game or around a plate of cheese (yes, before a meal!), no excuse is needed for a beer or two among friends.

FRUIT KETCHUPS

Contrary to what one might think, ketchup is not an American invention, courtesy of Mr Heinz, but quite simply a savory sweet-and-sour sauce that goes perfectly with grilled meat. In Montreal, fruit ketchup has become a real institution. Every self-respecting family prepares its conserves for the year ahead. The recipes are very varied, but often consist of a base of tomatoes, onions and celery, mixed with one or more fruits (apples, peaches, pears, and so forth). This sweet and savory blend is truly delicious. Instead of making it yourself, you can seek out numerous varieties at the Marché des Saveurs du Québec (see p. 60).

Cinema

Apart from certain celebrated films, such as *The Decline of the American Empire* or, more recently, *The Barbaric Invasions*, Quebec cinema is not very well known outside Canada. It is with some surprise, therefore, that one learns that the art of film-making is one of the most flourishing industries of the city.

CINÉMATHÈQUE
QUÉBÉCOISE
335, boul. De Maisonneuve Est
MédiaSphère Bell
Centre NAD
Alliance numériQC
Phonothèque québéroise
Restaurant

A real industry

Endowed with the biggest film-studio complex in Canada, Montreal is up there among other significant North American cities for movie production. Several thousand highly qualified technicians in the diverse realms of cinematography, set construction and special effects make their living in the industry here.
The city's reputation for motion-picture production is well established, and foreign companies are increasingly turning up to make their films here. This is the case for many American movies, such as Roland Emmerich's *The Day After Tomorrow* or Steven Spielberg's *The Terminal*.

Natural sets

The city's architecture allows it to play a great variety of roles. Old Montreal with its European charm and its buildings from the

FESTIVALS

Montreal couldn't be considered a movie town unless it staged some big public events. Among nearly 20 film festivals held in the city, Le Rendezvous du Cinéma Québécois (in February) celebrates the work of local artists, while the Montreal World Film Festival (August) is a large-scale enterprise presenting movies from about 70 countries in competition, and the International Festival of New Cinema and New Media (October) turns the spotlight on director's cinema and digital creations.

Information:
www.rvcq.com ☎ (514) 526 9635
www.ffm-montreal.org ☎ (514) 848 3883
www.fcmm.com ☎ (514) 847 9272

8th and 19th centuries, s ultramodern downtown kyscrapers, akin to those f the great American netropolises, and especially s many nature parks, llow the city to transform self according to the emands of the scenario. t can become New York or erlin for *Confessions of a Dangerous Man,* Moscow or *The Sum of All Fears,* or ven New Delhi in *The Day fter Tomorrow.*

Digital technology

n 1986, the director Daniel anglois launched a evolution in 3-D animation y creating the Softimage oftware. Since then, in esponse to the boundless assion of young people for nultimedia, Montreal has ontinued to give birth to ompanies specializing n the processing of digital magery. In consequence, Montreal has been propelled o the position of global eader in the production of pecial-effects software. t is thanks to these Quebec rograms (Softimage, Discreet, Toon Boom Technologies, Kaydara and Miranda) that films such as *Titanic, Jurassic Park, Godzilla* and *The Matrix* have seen the light of day. Its mastery of advanced technology has similarly conferred upon Montreal an important role in the creation of video games.

Denys Arcand, "infant prodigy"

A worthy representative of Quebec cinema, Denys Arcand knows how to broach painful topics without plunging into outright melodrama, and how to leaven his material with lightness and humor.
After working for the National Film Board of Canada, he made many feature-length movies that drew international applause, such as *The Decline of the American Empire, Jesus of Montreal* and, most recently, *The Barbaric Invasions.* The latter was indeed apotheosized in 2004 when it won the Oscar for the best foreign film, as well as three Caesars (best film, best screenplay and best director) and two prizes at the Cannes Festival the previous year.
Less renowned on an international level, but key players in Quebec cinema, directors Gilles Carle and Claude Jutra have both produced fine works (including *Mon Oncle Antoine*), which may be seen at the CinéRobothèque (see p. 57).

Underground city, indoor city

One of the unique features of Montreal and an integral part of its character, this huge network of underground galleries enables the city's downtown area to maintain its economic vitality throughout the year. It is reckoned to be the most extensive in the world – an ambitious, and ultimately successful, piece of urban planning.

Underground city or indoor city?

It's a sensible question to ask. By definition, an underground city must be laid out entirely below the earth's surface, implying the absence of natural light and an eventual feeling of enclosure. But here instead we find a network open to the outside, with about half the space being on ground level or higher. If this configuration has often been called an underground city, it's because its numerous shopping malls are connected to each other by long subterranean passages linked to subway stations. It is therefore possible to traverse a good part of the city without putting a foot outdoors. This is why nowadays some Montrealers refer to it, more accurately perhaps, as the "indoor city."

Construction

Its development was intrinsically linked to the construction of the subway system and the erection of modern skyscrapers. Born from a visionary urge to multiply tenfold the vitality of downtown Montreal, while at the same time acknowledging the rigors of the climate, the beginning of the underground development coincided with the construction of Place Ville-Marie from 1954 through 1962 (see p. 46). This cross-shaped tower of 47 stories was to be provided with an immense shopping mall in the basement. Then an adjacent subterranean excavation facilitated the creation of a tunnel linking the building to the central railroad station, and marking also the start of the indoor city. Since then, the network has grown exponentially, until today there are 20 miles of underground passageways linked to ten subway stations, 89 buildings, eight large hotels, two railroad stations, five universities and 2,727 apartments.

Getting one's bearings

There are no less than 178 entrances to this vast pedestrian network, but the simplest way in is via one of the relevant subway stations (Peel, McGill, Bonaventure, Place-d'Armes, and so on) or through one of the shopping malls that opens directly onto the street, such as the Desjardins Complex (see p. 53), the Eaton Center (see p. 121), or even the Montreal Trade Center (see p. 45). A word of advice: Get yourself a map of the indoor city from the tourist office. Even so, though armed with a map, once underground it's very easy to lose yourself. The direction panels don't refer to the streets outside but to the names of the shops and buildings linked by the network. Thus it's vital to know where you're going. But after one or two false starts you will soon get used to navigating your way around this amazing city with its octopus-like tentacles.

Shopper's paradise

Here is the rainbow's end for shoppers: a paradise on earth! It will take you an eternity to explore the more than one thousand shops of the indoor city. The days are well and truly over when rain, snow and blizzard or the dog days of high summer could thwart the pleasures of the dedicated window-shopper. Montreal can from now on boast of having mastered the vagaries of its climate and boosted its commercial activity. And you will find a multitude of cafés and lunch counters where you can pause for a breather. The Eaton Center is the biggest of these shopping malls, and this would be a good starting point for your underground adventure. Since it is the epicenter of the indoor pedestrian axis that runs the length of Rue Sainte-Catherine, it will allow you to access Cours Mont-Royal and Place Montréal Trust (west side), as well as the Les Ailes complex, the La Baie shopping area (east side), McGill University (center) and Place Ville-Marie (south side). Have a good journey.

THE SUBWAY

Opened in 1966, Montreal's subway system could be considered one of the curiosities of the city. Each station (out of 65) is unique, its decor surrendered to the imagination of the architects and artists who designed it. There you will find frescoes, mosaics, glasswork and sculptures that remind you that the subway forms an integral part of the originality and distinctiveness of this vast network of underground galleries.

The performing arts

While it's true that Montreal can pride itself on the quality of its dance companies, such as the Grands Ballets Canadiens, and on its theater productions (see p. 138), it is also the starting point of several sectors of the performing arts that have made a name for themselves at an international level.

Humor

Montreal's famous comedy scene has launched many brilliant careers. With its own school, its own museum (see p. 54) and its famous festival, humor has become an art. On the back of the colossal success of the Just for Laughs Festival (see p. 21), the École Nationale d'Humour opened its doors in 1988. Offering both a program of creative humor aimed at humorists and a writing program designed for authors, the school has graduated many of today's foremost Quebec comedians, such as Martin Matte, Peter MacLeod and Laurent Paquin. This urge to make people laugh reflects the love of performance and of life itself that animates Montrealers.

Theatrical improvisation

In 1977, the actor, author and director Robert Gravel founded the National League of Improvisation. The concept of theatrical "improvisation matches" rapidly took hold. The principle is very simple. Two teams of comedians confront each other on stage, improvising scenes on subjects drawn at random and imposed by a referee. The two teams perform one after the other, according to strict rules, and the public has to decide between them. Today there are several leagues throughout the world where such matches have become regular theatrical gatherings. In Montreal, the season runs from February through May.

Information:
☎ (514) 528 5430 or www.lni.ca

Le Cirque du Soleil

In 1984, a group of street artists (musicians, jugglers, fire-eaters, and so on) was given the opportunity to put on a show to celebrate the 450th anniversary of the discovery of Canada. They called the spectacle "le Cirque du Soleil" (the Circus of the Sun). Founded in Montreal by Guy Laliberté, this troupe of artists of every kind continued to grow until it blossomed into an international company of 3,000 employees from across the globe. Their shows are spectacular and magical, incorporating acrobatics, dance, martial arts, multimedia and pyrotechnics. Faithful to the land of its birth, the company maintains its headquarters in Montreal, contributing to the status of the city. Le Cirque du Soleil is accommodated in the Cité des Arts du Cirque (Circus Arts Complex), managed by TOHU (www.tohu.ca).

Storytelling

Less theatrical, but equally a vehicle for communication, storytelling is a Quebec tradition going back many decades. To help preserve and promote this art form, Montreal hosts, in October each year, the Quebec Intercultural Festival of Storytelling, an event based on the swapping and sharing of storytelling techniques, during which narrators, like travelers, recount stories and incidents full of wit and sensitivity (information: ☎ (514) 272 4494 or www.festival-conte.qc.ca). And, to meet an ever-increasing demand, the city has played host, since 2003, to a second gathering entitled the "Festival de Conte de Bouche à l'Oreille" (Festival of Intimate Storytelling). In addition, there are several bars that organize evening sessions dedicated to this art throughout the year.

GREAT VOCALISTS

Montreal, and Quebec generally, have given birth to a large number of artists whose voices have traveled across the Atlantic. From Robert Charlebois to Garou, by way of Diane Tell, Isabelle Boulay, Natasha Saint-Pier and, of course, Celine Dion, the singers of Quebec, influenced by Anglo-Saxon culture, possess a powerful vocal talent and an innate sense of rhythm. Those who prefer vocals with a poetic texture will enjoy listening to the cult songs of Gilles Vigneault and Richard Desjardins, two of the singer-songwriters who contribute to Quebec's continuing vocal tradition.

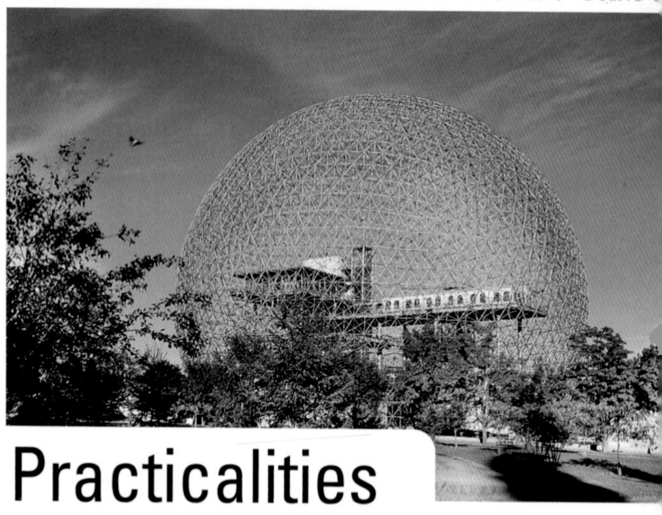

Practicalities

Getting around

On foot

To get to know this city, there's no better way than to explore it on foot. Downtown and Old Montreal being so close to each other, it's easy to walk between them, and that will allow you discover characteristic corners like the Chinese quarter. From the Old Town, you soon enter the Latin Quarter, at Boulevard Saint-Laurent and Plateau Mont-Royal. In short, as you may already have figured, except for certain outlying areas such as Westmount, Outremont, Little Italy, or, to be sure, Olympic Park, it's best to put on a good pair of shoes and – as long as your energy lasts – walk! To give you an idea of the distances involved, it will take you about 20 minutes to go up Rue Sainte-Catherine from Rue Berri to Rue Peel, without counting stopovers for shopping, of course!

FINDING YOUR WAY

Montreal has an extensive metro (subway) system (see text for detail). We have included details of the nearest metro station throughout this guide by using the symbol M° followed by the name of the station.

By subway

The subway network comprises four lines, three spreading out from Parc du Mont-Royal, and the fourth linking Île de Montréal with Parc Jean-Drapeau. Differentiated by color, they operate every day at the following times:

Green and orange lines:
Sun.-Fri. 5.30-0.30am,
Sat. 5.30-1.00am

Yellow line:
Sun.-Fri. 5.30-1.00am,
Sat. 5.30-1.30am

Blue line:
Mon.-Sun. 5.30-0.15am.

A night bus service provides transportation after the last subway trains.
Tickets are sold at every station. They can be bought singly ($2.50) or in a carnet (booklet) of six ($11).
You can also buy a card for unlimited weekly travel (CAM Hebdo), beginning Mondays ($18).
Children under 5 travel for free, and those from 6 to 11 at a reduced price.
Conveniently, the subway is also at the hub of the indoor city. The downtown stations allow you direct access to the different shopping malls, and it will sometimes be easier for you to find these entrances than to find the way out to the surface!

By bus

The bus drivers don't sell tickets, so you have to buy them in advance. The same tickets and carnets are used for both the buses and the subway. If you buy a single ticket and your journey requires a transfer (from subway to bus, for example), be sure to ask for a *billet de correspondance* (transfer ticket). They are obtainable at subway stations and from bus drivers, and will save you having to buy several tickets for a single journey. Buses follow roughly the same schedule as the subway, but there is also a night service that operates from midnight through 5am. You can pick up a general map of the network as well as maps for individual lines from the Berri-UQAM subway station.

By cab

After a hard day's walking, it might be more agreeable to travel by cab when night falls. They are fairly plentiful and relatively cheap (it's unusual for a ride in the downtown area to come to more than $10). You can flag them in the street (the most effective way), take them at a taxicab rank, or telephone for one. Avoid paying in large bills, and don't forget to give a tip.

Taxi Diamond
☎ (514) 273 6331.
Champlain Taxi
☎ (514) 273 2435.

By car

Unless you want to make some excursions outside Montreal, it is really not necessary to hire a car for your visit. Downtown parking is expensive (up to $2 an hour at a meter, and about $5 in a parking lot), and, in addition, you will need all your patience to decipher the parking-regulation signs. If you do need to rent a car, you must be

READING MAPS

If you look at a map for the whole of the isle, Montreal will seem very big, and difficult to cover in one weekend. But don't worry, for in speaking of Montreal only the center of the city with its four surrounding areas (clustered in the south, the east and north-west of Parc du Mont-Royal) is meant. Boulevard Saint-Laurent (which crosses the whole island from south to north) is an essential artery, dividing the east and west sides of the city. All the streets that intersect with it indicate whether they are "Est" (east) or "Ouest" (west), shown by the initials "E" or "O" on maps, allowing you easily to orient yourself. Thus Rue Sainte-Catherine Est is right of Boulevard Saint-Laurent, and Rue Sainte-Catherine Ouest is left of it. The numbering of these streets also begins at Boulevard Saint-Laurent. So the lower the numbers are, the closer they are to the boulevard. As for the streets oriented on the north–south axis, their numbering begins at the St Lawrence River. There are instances of two or more street sharing the same name, so bear this in mind when using a map index.

over 21, have held your driver's license for more than a year, and be able to produce a credit card. Note also that the vast majority of cars have automatic transmission.

Avis
1225, rue Metcalfe
M° Peel
☎ (514) 866 7906.
Hertz
1073, rue Drummond
M° Bonaventure
☎ (514) 938 1717.
Pelletier
3585, rue Berri
M° Sherbrooke
☎ (514) 281 5000.

By bicycle and motor scooter

Montreal has numerous cycle tracks, the bicycle being a favored form of transport once the fine weather arrives. Not only is it a pleasant means of transit, but the bicycle allows you to make some very pleasant excursions: beside the Lachine Canal (see p. 68), for example, along the promenade of the Vieux-Port (see p. 43), or, for the more athletic, around Parc du Mont-Royal (see pp. 64 and 81). You are also allowed to take a bicycle on the subway, all day on weekends and holidays, and between 10am and 3pm and after 7pm on weekdays. To do that, you have to be over 16 (or accompanied by an adult), and travel in the first subway car, at the front of the train. To hire a bicycle will cost between $7 and $7.50 an hour, or between $22 and $25 for the day. To obtain a map of cycle tracks, go to the tourist office (see the next page) or La Maison des Cyclistes (see p. 59).

Ça roule Montréal
27, rue de la Commune Est
M° Champ-de-Mars
☎ (514) 866 0633
www.caroulemontreal.com
Vélo Aventure Montréal
Quai des Convoyeurs, Vieux-Port
M° Place-d'Armes
☎ (514) 847 0666
www.veloaventure.com
Alex Berthiaume et fils
4398, rue de la Roche
☎ (514) 521 0230
www.alexberthiaume.com
Berthiaume is a specialist in motor scooters and similar vehicles.

Communications

The telephone

The area code for Montreal is ☎ 514, but you don't have to use it when you're there. The code for Greater Montreal, outside the island of Montreal, is ☎ 450. Although it is considered a local call, this code must be dialed if it forms part of the number you're calling. From outside North America, you must use the prefix 1, the international code for Canada. So, to call Montreal from the UK, you must dial 00 1 514 followed by the number. Conversely, to call the UK from Canada, you have to dial ☎ 011 44 followed by the number, but without the 0. Numbers beginning with ☎ (800), ☎ (866), ☎ (877) and ☎ (888) are free. In Montreal, the telephone is user-friendly. For 25 cents you can call a local number from a public telephone and talk as

USEFUL INFORMATION

US consulate:
1155, rue St-Alexandre
☎ (514) 398 9695.
British consulate:
1000, rue de la Gauchetière
☎ (514) 866 5863.
Emergency: (fire/police/ambulance)
☎ 911
Quebec Poisons Center:
☎ 1 (800) 463 5060
Weather forecasts:
☎ (514) 283 3010

CARTE MUSÉES MONTRÉAL

The Montreal museum card is a passport giving access to thirty museums and places of interest in Montreal and its neighborhood, as well as to the public transit system (bus and subway). This card is valid for three days and costs $39 (including tax). It is sold in the ticket offices of museums, in certain hotels and at the tourist office. For a great weekend, this makes everything straightforward. Take advantage of it! Information: www.museesmontreal.org

long as you like. If you want to call long distance, the simplest method is to buy a prepaid telephone card from any newsstand, convenience store or drugstore (see pp. 101 and 36). Make sure to check the tariffs in force at the place you wish to telephone from. Check the rates at your hotel, especially, as they may be unexpectedly high.

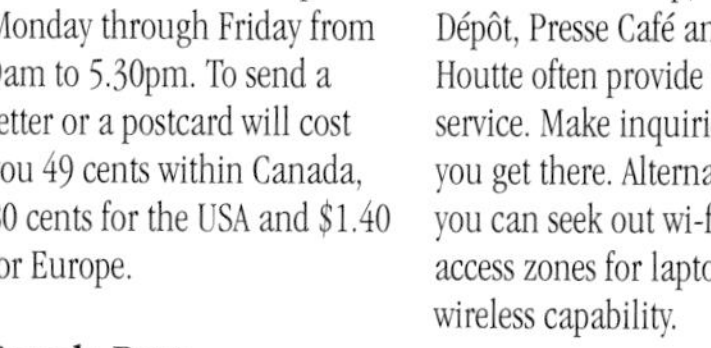

Post office

You can buy postage stamps at any post office and most drugstores and convenience stores. Post offices are open Monday through Friday from 9am to 5.30pm. To send a letter or a postcard will cost you 49 cents within Canada, 80 cents for the USA and $1.40 for Europe.

Canada Post
☎ (800) 267 1177 (freephone).
Post Office
1695, rue Sainte-Catherine Est
M° Papineau
☎ (514) 522 3220.
Maison de la poste
(postal museum, gift shop and coin collection)
1250, rue University
M° McGill
☎ (514) 846 5401.

Internet

In case your hotel doesn't offer Internet facilities, there are numerous cybercafés. Connection is quick and will cost you about $3 for 30 minutes (the rates generally decrease the longer you are online). The coffee-shop chains Second Cup, Café Dépôt, Presse Café and Van Houtte often provide this service. Make inquiries when you get there. Alternatively, you can seek out wi-fi Internet access zones for laptops with wireless capability.

Presse Café
1750, rue Saint-Denis
M° Sherbrooke
☎ (514) 847 1389.
MBCO
1447, rue Stanley
M° Peel
☎ (514) 284 0404.
Café Dépôt
1490, bd de Maisonneuve Ouest
M° Guy Concordia
☎ (514) 931 1570.

Currency exchange

Most banks will change foreign currency and cash traveler's checks. They are open Monday through Friday from 10am to 3pm (some stay open until 6pm Thursdays and Fridays). Outside of these hours, you can go to one of the foreign exchange offices located downtown (several of them are sited along Rue Sainte-Catherine, at the Central Station (505, bd de Maisonneuve Est, M° Berri-UQAM), in Vieux-Montréal (rue Saint-Jacques) or at Montreal Casino, whose office is open 24 hours every day (see p. 73). Alternatively, you can of course withdraw money by using your bank card at any ATM. However, since your bank will often charge commission, it is better to withdraw one substantial amount rather than several smaller ones. And, if you want to spare yourself all this bother, provide yourself with plenty of Canadian dollars before coming.

Tourist office

For detailed information and maps, you can visit the Website of the Montreal Tourist Office: www.tourisme-montreal.org

Bureau d'accueil touristique:
174, rue Notre-Dame Est
M° Champ-de-Mars
☎ (514) 874 1696
Mon.-Sun. (variable hours).
Centre Infotouriste:
1255, rue Peel, bureau 100
M° Peel
☎ (514) 873 2015
Mon.-Sun. 8.30am-7.30pm

(Jun. 1 through Sep. 6), 9am-6pm (Sep. 7 through May 31).

Museum hours

Most museums open their doors at 10am or 11am, and close at 5pm. Many are closed on Mondays, but some of them, such as Musée des Beaux-Arts or Pointe-à-Callière, are open seven days a week in summer. The hours can vary from season to season; you need to check beforehand. Moreover, certain establishments, such as the art museums, have an evening opening (generally Wednesdays) until 9pm, at a reduced tariff or for free. Most of the museums are also open on public holidays.

CONVENIENCE STORES

If you want to nibble something en route, try a convenience store (*dépanneur*). Similar to the famous New York delicatessens, they are general stores, with unassuming fronts, whose sole aim is simply to help you out and keep you going. You will find everything you need; they stay open till late at night, as indicated by the name of one of their chains, "Couche-Tard" (Late Sleeper).

Organized tours

For those of you who are seeking another way of discovering Montreal, whether for the knowledge that a professional guide can impart, or perhaps looking for something a bit more exciting, here are some organizations that may be of service:

By bus

Autobus Viens / Impérial Centre Infotouriste
1001, square Dorchester
M° Peel
☎ (514) 871 4733
www.bus-viens.qc.ca
Fares from $31 to $35 per adult.
There are several alternatives for touring the city, with stops or without, by luxury bus or London bus. The tour can last three hours or be spread over two days, depending on how much time you have available.

By bicycle

Ça roule Montréal
(see the information on p. 34)
Tariffs vary according to the option chosen. In addition to simply renting bicycles, this organization offers guided tours in scenic landscapes such as the Lachine Canal, the isles of Notre-Dame and Sainte-Hélène, Mont-Royal, the Plateau, Olympic Park, and even Parc des Iles de Boucherville. The trips can cover anything from six to 24 miles. It's up to you to decide how long you can last!

By water

Le Bateau-Mouche (sightseeing boat)
Vieux-Port de Montréal
Quai Jacques-Cartier
M° Champ-de-Mars
☎ (514) 849 9952
www.bateau-mouche.com
Mid-May through mid-Oct.
Tariffs vary according to the option chosen.
This excursion aboard a *bateau-mouche* will enable you to visit places inaccessible to traditional boats. You will see the Lachine Canal and its locks, pass by the islands of the Saint-Laurent and approach the Sainte-Marie current. There are six sailings daily, including a magnificent dinner cruise (departing at 7pm).

L'Amphi-Bus
Vieux-Port de Montréal
M° Champ-de-Mars
☎ (514) 849 5181
May through Oct.
Fare about $21 per adult.
An amphibious waterbus offers you two different experiences, with a guided tour of the Old Town and a visit to the Old Port (on the St Lawrence River, but by water!

Les Descentes du Saint-Laurent (St Lawrence rapids)
8912, bd La Salle, LaSalle
☎ (514) 284 9607
M° Angrignon then bus no. 110
www.raftingmontreal.com
May through Sep.
Fares from $38 to $45 per adult.
Located in the LaSalle district this organization provides

rips by raft or jet boat on the Lachine rapids. Adventure lovers are in for a treat. The gear is provided; take only a change of clothing.

Les Expéditions sur les Rapides de Lachine (Expeditions on Lachine rapids)
Vieux-Port, quai de l'Horloge
M° Champ-de-Mars
☎ (514) 284 9607
www.jetboatingmontreal.com
May through Oct.
Fares from $22 to $55 per adult.
If wild water doesn't scare you, climb aboard one of these powerful jet boats for a game of leapfrog on the Lachine rapids, or for a high-speed ride with sideslips and 360° bends on the St Lawrence. Shooting the rapids by raft is also on the menu.

By air

Delco Aviation
☎ (450) 663 4311
www.delcoaviation.com
Discover magical landscapes on board a hydroplane. You can fly over Montreal in 20 minutes, or spend a little longer to discover the Laurentides wildlife reserve, Niagara Falls or even the Great North!

Air Limo Canada
4800, route de l'Aéroport, Saint-Hubert
☎ (450) 656 5688
www.airlimocanada.com
This company offers panoramic flights over the city of Montreal and the Laurentides aboard small propeller planes. You can also ask for details of the night flights offered.

Themed tours

Guidatour
477, rue Saint-François-Xavier, bureau 300
M° Place-d'Armes
☎ (514) 844 4021
www.guidatour.qc.ca
This company offers a multitude of ways to see

the city: a guide companion, a guide personality (a historic personage brought to life), bus tours or cycle trips. Various other themes are available, such as: "The City of Julie Papineau," "The Golden Square Mile of Lady Bartholomew" or even "The World of Michel Tremblay on a Plate." It's an original way of having a history lesson and the kids will enjoy it.

Architectours – Héritage Montréal
☎ (514) 286 2662
www.heritagemontreal.qc.ca
Summer season only
Fare: $12 per adult.
Architectours are walks based on historical or architectural themes and on the development of different areas of the city. Numerous sites are included. Each visit lasts about two hours.

Circuit des Fantômes du Vieux-Montréal (Ghost Tour of Old Montreal)
Promenade du Vieux-Port (level: quai Jacques-Cartier)
M° Champ-de-Mars or Place-d'Armes
☎ (514) 868-0303
www.phvm.qc.ca
Jun. through Aug.
Tickets on sale from 6.30pm.
Fare: $15 per adult.
As night falls, these ghost tours bring Old Montreal back to life with the help of three eerie itineraries: "Ghost hunting in New France" (Fri.), "Historic crimes of Montreal" (Thu. and Sat.) and "Legends of Old Montreal" (Wed. and Sun.). Goose bumps are guaranteed.

VOLTAGE, WEIGHTS AND MEASURES

As everywhere in North America, the electrical current is 110 volts. You must therefore bring a plug adapter with you if you want to use European electrical appliances. In addition, Canada adopted the metric system some time ago, though many people still talk in terms of miles, feet and inches.
It may be useful to keep in mind certain equivalents:
1 inch = 2.54 cm
1 foot = about 30 cm
1 mile = about 1.6 km

What to see in Montreal and sights not to miss

To help you discover the city, we suggest 17 walks in Montreal, with a map for each one, plus a walk on the outskirts. If you don't have much time, here is a selection of 10 attractions that you should make every effort to see before you leave. They are all mentioned elsewhere in this guidebook, and you will find specific information about them at the end of this section (Don't Miss, pp. 76-85).

St Joseph's Oratory

Truly a treasure of religious architecture, St Joseph's Oratory is one of the most popular sites in Montreal.

See walk 13, p. 64 and Don't Miss p. 76.

Museum of Contemporary Art

The work of Paul-Émile Borduas, which marked a turning point in the artistic history of Quebec, is showcased here.

See walk 7, p. 52 and Don't Miss p. 77.

Musée des Beaux-Arts (Museum of Fine Arts)

A visit to the museum, one of the largest in North America, is not to be missed.

See walk 6, p. 50 and Don't Miss p. 78.

Renoir, *Young Girl in a Hat*

Centre d'Histoire (Montreal History Center)

The perfect place to learn about the history of the city in an entertaining way.

See walk 2, p. 42 and Don't Miss p. 79.

Jardin Botanique (Botanical Garden)

Here devotees of nature will find thousands of plant species without having to go round the world.

See walk 16, p. 70 and Don't Miss p. 80

Parc du Mont-Royal (Mont-Royal Park)

Climb to the summit and have the beauty of Montreal engraved in your memory for ever.

See walk 13, p. 64 and Don't Miss p. 81

Plateau Mont-Royal

Here you can saunter at leisure along streets of timeless charm. Unforgettable!

See walk 10, p. 58 and Don't Miss p. 82.

Pointe-à-Callière

An authentic archeological site displaying more than a thousand years of history.

See walk 2, p. 42 and Don't Miss p. 83

Vieux-Port (Old Port)

Many leisure activities are brought together in one spot. If you want to relax, this is the place.

See walk 2, p. 42 and Don't Miss p. 84.

Basilique Notre-Dame (Notre Dame Basilica)

This sparkling jewel of Catholic architecture won't disappoint you. Judge for yourself.

See walk 3, p. 44 and Don't Miss p. 85

1

Old Montreal, from the east side

Cobbled streets, *calèches* (horse-drawn carriages) and buildings of a bygone era lend Vieux-Montreal something of a European air. Wander round here by day, to take in some of the time-worn edifices that you can rediscover at night bathed in floodlights. It's magic.

❶ Place Jacques-Cartier★★

Laid out in 1804 on the site of the former Château de Vaudreuil, this famous sloping square is named in honor of Jacques Cartier, the discoverer of Canada in 1534. In summer, the atmosphere here is reminiscent of Montmartre: the terraces of cafés and restaurants look out on a crowd of artists of every description.

❷ Hôtel de Ville★ (City Hall)

275, rue Notre-Dame Est
☎ (514) 872 3355.

This remarkable building of Second Empire style was constructed between 1872 and 1878 by Henri-Maurice Perrault. After a terrible fire in 1922, the interior and the roof were completely rebuilt in the style of the *mairie* (town hall) of Tours, in France. The new City Hall was opened in 1926, and it was from its balcony that General de Gaulle proclaimed, in 1967, his famous slogan, "Vive le Québec libre" ("Long live free Quebec").

❸ Musée du Château Ramezay★★

280, rue Notre-Dame Est
☎ (514) 861 3708
www.chateauramezay.qc.ca
Jun. 1-Sep. 30 Mon.-Fri. 10am-6pm; Oct. 1-May 31 Tue.-Sun. 10am-4.30pm
Admission charge.

Erected in 1705 for the governor of Montreal, Claude de Ramezay, this splendid

residence only received its official title of "Château" in 1903. Having housed the East India Company and several governors general, the building has been, since 1895, the oldest private museum of Quebec history. Among its 30,000 artifacts, there is a remarkable Amerindian ethnology section and an outstanding collection of coins. An enclosed garden, in 18th-century style, has been laid out in the back courtyard.

❹ Marché Bonsecours★★ (Bonsecours Market)

350, rue Saint-Paul Est
☎ (514) 872 7730
www.marchebonsecours.qc.ca
Open every day at varying times, depending on the season.

Opened in 1847, this neoclassical building with its silvery, almost 100ft dome has housed, in turn, the United Canada Parliament, Montreal City Hall and a public market. In 1963, the building closed its doors to all, and it wasn't until 1996 that Bonsecours Market sprung back to life. Today boutiques selling the original creations of Quebec craftspeople and designers find a home here.

❺ Chapelle Notre-Dame-de-Bonsecours and Musée Marguerite-Bourgeoys★★

400, rue Saint-Paul Est; ☎ (514) 282 8670; www.marguerite-bourgeoys.com
Museum: May-Oct, Tue.-Sun. 10am-5.30pm; Nov-Jan and Mar-Apr, Tue.-Sun. 11am-3.30pm; closed mid-Jan.-end Feb
Chapel open all year round. Free admission to chapel, charge for the museum.

It was at the request of Marguerite Bourgeoys, a French nun and schoolteacher, that this chapel dedicated to the Virgin Mary was built between 1657 and 1675. Montreal's first stone-built church, it is a place of pilgrimage for sailors (as witnessed by the commemorative plaques in the form of model ships hanging in the nave). The museum traces the history of the church and the life of its founder. Each afternoon in summer, a dramatization in the crypt brings back to life famous personalities of the era.

❻ 12° en cave★★

367, rue Saint-Paul Est
☎ (514) 866 5722
www.12encave.com
Mon.-Sat. 10am-8pm, Sun. 10am-6pm.

A space given over entirely to wine! Whatever vintage you might be seeking, or whatever useful or decorative accessory, this place is a real gold mine: wall-mounted corkscrews, thermometers, hygrometers, Victorian funnels. On the ornamental side, you'll find some superb marble slabs silk-screened with labels of famous wines. And to finish with, the famous Vino Quizz (wine quiz), a kind of Trivial Pursuit for wine buffs.

❼ LE CABARET DU ROY★

If the idea of tasting food from the 18th century appeals to you, take your place at the table of your choice and partake of a spectacular dinner. You will begin, no doubt, with a *sagamité*, an Amerindian corn and fish-flavored soup that will knock out the weakest stomachs right at the start! If the portions are too vast, a menu à la carte can be requested. A festive atmosphere is guaranteed!

363, rue de la Commune Est
☎ (514) 907 9000; www.oyez.ca
Mon.-Sun. 11.30am-11pm.

2

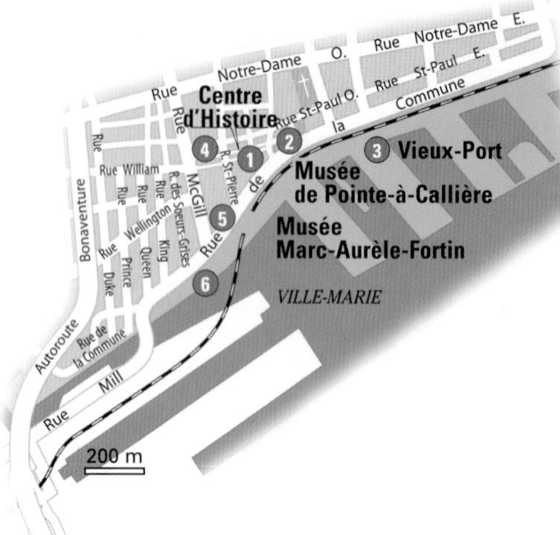

The cradle of history, from the west side

It was at Pointe-à-Callière that Chomedey de Maisonneuve founded Ville-Marie in 1642. A true cradle of history, a visit to this part of Vieux-Montréal lets you experience the soul of the city. The Rue Saint-Paul and the former stables of Place d'Youville encourage a friendly village atmosphere.

❶ Centre d'Histoire de Montréal★★★

335, place d'Youville
☎ (514) 872 3207
www.ville.montreal.qc.ca/chm
May-Aug., Tue.-Sun. 10am-5pm; Sep.-Apr., Wed.-Sun. 10am-5pm
Admission charge
See Don't Miss p. 79.

This is the place where you will find the most comprehensive history of Montreal. Installed in a former fire station, this cultural center will take you through the evolution of the city, from its foundation to the present day.

Focusing at the same time on crucial historical events and the daily life of the inhabitants, it will provide you with an excellent understanding of the city.

❷ Pointe-à-Callière, musée d'Archéologie et d'Histoire de Montréal★★★

350, place Royale
☎ (514) 872 9150
www.pacmusee.qc.ca
Mon.-Fri. 10am-5pm
Sat.-Sun. 11am-5pm (until 6pm in Jul. and Aug.)
Admission charge.
See Don't Miss p. 83.

Opened in 1992, this archeology and history museum is the result of more than ten years of archeological excavation. Erected on the very spot where the city was founded – the Pointe-à-

6 CAFÉ DES ÉCLUSIERS★

Located on the banks of the St Lawrence River, Café des Éclusiers – "Lock-keepers' Café" – certainly possesses the most highly prized summer terrace. With its round outdoor bar right on the water's edge, and rattan armchairs and parasols, it will leave you in no doubt that you are truly on vacation. Light or grilled meals enjoyed in the sunshine, delicious tapas from 5pm onwards, themed dinner evenings: the choice is yours! The liveliest soirées often take place on Thursdays.

Intersection of av McGill and rue de la Commune Ouest; ☎ (514) 496 0762; www.cafedeseclusiers.com Mon.-Wed. 11am-11pm, Thu. 11am-1am, Fri.-Sun. 11am-midnight.

Callière – it has on display the remains that bear witness to the origins of Montreal. In addition to the archeological crypt located underground, the museum also features, just above the ruins, an exceptional multimedia display on the history of the city.

3 Vieux-Port de Montréal★★★

www.vieuxportdemontreal.com; see Don't Miss p. 84.

Made the official port of entry into Canada in 1830, the Old Port today offers a pleasant promenade beside the St Lawrence River. Extensive development has resulted in the provision of numerous sporting, cultural and recreational amenities. Among these are the Shed 16 Labyrinth and the Science Center, equipped with a giant Imax screen. From May to September, special events are organized: concerts, open-air movies, children's shows, tango lessons, and so on.

4 Espace Pepin★★

350, rue Saint-Paul Ouest
☎ (514) 844 0114
www.pepinart.com
Mon.-Sat. 10am-7pm, Sun. 11am-6pm.

The bright idea for this boutique-gallery-apartment in the heart of Vieux-Montréal came from Lysanne Pepin. The canvases of this painter – nudes and portraits conveying an amazing sensuality – are interspersed among other objects, clothes and accessories created by artists and artisans, very pleasing to the eye. Lysanne Pepin also offers reproductions of her paintings on canvas, as well as T-shirts printed with her works (about $50).

5 Musée Marc-Aurèle-Fortin★★

118, rue Saint-Pierre
☎ (514) 854 6108
www.museemafortin.org
Tue.-Sun. 11am-5pm
Admission charge.

A little gallery entirely devoted to the work of this artist, with more than 90 paintings. Born in 1888 north of Montreal, Marc-Aurèle Fortin is regarded as the foremost Canadian landscape painter. Admired for the brilliant luminosity of certain of his paintings, he made use of various techniques, such as watercolor sponge and natural watercolor. Throughout the gallery, detailed information panels shed light on his lesser-known works.

3

Around
Rue Saint-Jacques

Former symbol of financial muscle, Rue Saint-Jacques separates the Old Town from the recently developed "international quarter." The latter contains bold contemporary structures such as the Palais des Congrès and the Centre de Commerce Mondial (Montreal World Trade Centre). On the other side of the street looms the basilique Notre-Dame, another image of power, this time religious.

❶ Basilique Notre-Dame de Montréal★★★

110, rue Notre-Dame Ouest
☎ (514) 842 2925
www.basiliquenddm.org
Mon.-Fri. 8am-4.30pm,
Sat. 8am-4.15pm,
Sun. 12.30-4.15pm
Admission charge
See Don't Miss p. 85.

Built between 1824 and 1829, the basilica is one of the principal works of Neo-Gothic architecture bequeathed to us by James O'Donnell, a Protestant Irish architect. The interior decor, the work of Victor Bourgeau, is entirely of sculpted wood, adorned with paint and gold leaf. The magnificent stained-glass windows illustrate the history of the parish and Montreal society. Towards the back the Chapelle du Sacré-Coeur (Sacred Heart Chapel) has a more modern design.

❷ Place d'Armes★

Used formerly for military drill, Place d'Armes is in some respects a symbol of Montreal's history. In 1895, a statue was erected here in honor of Paul Chomedey de Maisonneuve, the city's founder. He is accompanied by other sculpted notables of that era: Jeanne Mance and Lambert Closse, both classed as original

›unders. Another historic ‹mbol is the old St Sulpice ›eminary, located next to the asilica. Constructed between 584 and 1687, it's the oldest uilding in Montreal, and :ill inhabited.

❸ Banque le Montréal★

19, rue Saint-Jacques
☎ (514) 877 6810

Mon.-Fri. 10am-4pm
ree admission.

ounded in 1817, this is the ldest bank in the country. 'he building was constructed 1 1847, in imitation of the 'antheon in Rome. The nterior, refurbished in 1905, oasts a splendid banking hall, eflecting the power of the nstitution. A small museum lisplays old banknotes, cash oxes and historic documents lating from the 19th century.

❹ Banque Royale★★

360, rue Saint-Jacques
☎ (514) 874 2959
Mon.-Fri. 10am-4pm

3uilt in 1928 and designed by New York architects York and 3awyer, the new headquarters of the Royal Bank, 23 stories high, was then the tallest office building in the British Empire. Occupying a complete city block, the institution wished to emphasize its strength and status as the largest bank in Canada. The ceilings are more than 40ft high; the interior decor, with its chandeliers, is majestic.

❼ PALAIS DES CONGRÈS★

Its imposing façade of colored glass is certain to attract your notice. Opened in 2002, the new Convention Center building aspired to become a showcase of modernity and a symbol of the "international quarter." Inside is an unusual sculpture garden, consisting of 52 pink tree-trunks, copied from the trees along Avenue du Parc.

1001, place Jean-Paul Riopelle
☎ (514) 871 8122
www.congresmtl.com

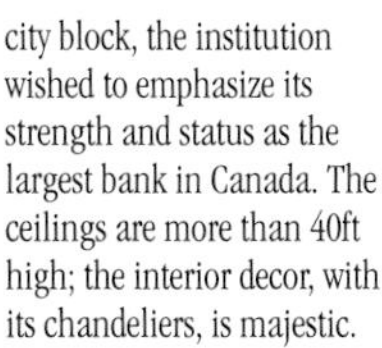

❺ Centre de Commerce Mondial de Montréal★★

747, rue du Square-Victoria
☎ (514) 982 9888
www.centredecommerce mondial.com

Something of an architectural marvel, the World Trade Center was constructed in 1992 on both sides of Ruelle des Fortifications. The remains of several old buildings were incorporated into the structure.

The *ruelle*, or alley (following the line of the ramparts of the 18th-century city), is covered by a glass roof. The Center contains more than 20 boutiques, restaurants and cafés, as well as a chunk of the Berlin Wall, given to the city on its 350th anniversary. The goddess of the sea, Amphitrite, at the edge of a water feature formerly adorned the municipal fountain in Saint-Mihiel, France.

❻ Toqué!★★★

900, place Jean-Paul-Riopelle
☎ (514) 499 2084
www.restaurant-toque.com
Tue.-Fri. 11.30am-2pm and 5.30-10.30pm, Sat. 5.30-10.30pm.

Considered one of the best eating places in Montreal, the Toqué! restaurant welcomes you in a modern setting, with a cuisine both imaginative and refined, emphasizing local Quebec produce (duck foie gras and Estrie lamb will give your palate a night to remember). Also on the carte: a *menu dégustation surprise* (surprise tasting menu) comprising six dishes (about $80).

4

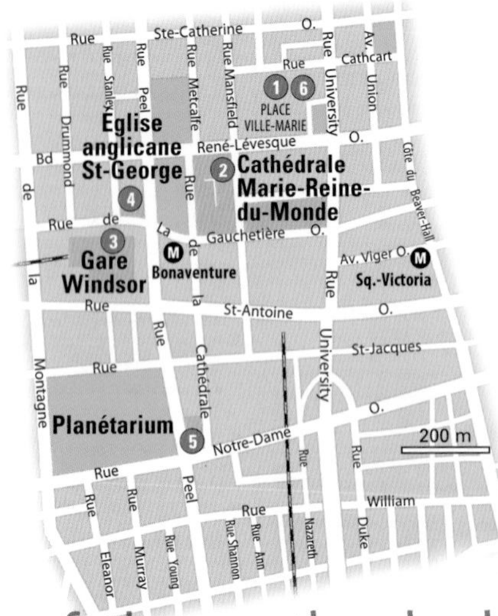

In the shadow of the cathedral

The modernity of skyscrapers, the beauty of religious buildings and the imposing architecture of Windsor Station form a unique landscape in this historic district. You'll find few stores on the surface, but underground they proliferate. The shopping mall at Place Ville-Marie is the hub of the vast indoor city network.

❶ Place Ville-Marie★

www.placevillemarie.com
Shopping mall:
Mon.-Wed. 9.30am-6pm,
Thu.-Fri. 9.30am-9pm,
Sat. 9.30am-5pm,
Sun. 12-5pm.

This cross-shaped skyscraper recalls the initial religious vocation of the city, dedicated to the Virgin Mary. Built towards the end of the 1950s to the design of the architect Ming Pei (who also designed the Louvre Pyramid in Paris), this complex comprises offices and extensive underground shopping malls, most of them linked to neighboring buildings. This structure marked the beginning of the underground city.

❷ Cathédrale Marie-Reine-du-Monde★★

1085, rue de la Cathédrale (intersection of rue Mansfield and bd René-Lévesque O.)
☎ (514) 866 1661
www.cathedralecatholiquedemontreal.org
Mon.-Sun. 6.30am-7pm.

After a horrific fire which destroyed the old Catholic cathedral in 1852, Monsignor Ignace Bourget decided that a replacement should be built in

❻ ALTITUDE 737★★★

Located on the 46th and highest story of the Place Ville-Marie tower, this restaurant, endowed with immense bay windows, provides the most beautiful panorama over the city that you can imagine. It's best to go there in the early evening, arriving as the sun sets. In a quiet, elegant setting, you can enjoy international cuisine. Each evening the carte offers different themed menus: French, Italian, Greek or Spanish (about $40 or $45 the menu). On a lower level is a lounge terrace for relaxation, and a night club.

Place Ville-Marie, Level PH2
☎ (514) 397 0737
www.altitude737.com
Tue.-Fri. noon-2pm, Tue.-Sat. 5.30-10.30pm.

the heart of the Protestant quarter, of grandiose proportions, surpassing those of the basilique Notre-Dame, and affirming the supremacy of the Catholic Church. Marie-Reine-du-Monde was therefore constructed between 1870 and 1894, modeled on St Peter's Basilica in Rome. Inside, an impressive Neo-Baroque baldachin dominates the nave.

❸ Windsor Station★

Intersection of rue Peel and rue de la Gauchetière Ouest.

With its massive Neo-Romanesque architecture, Windsor Station looks like a castle in the center of town. Opened in 1889 on the instructions of William Van Horne, director of the Canadian Pacific Railway, it became the business headquarters of the company and the linchpin of the Canadian railroad system. Today it provides space for shops and offices as well as the Bell Center, a stadium of more than 20,000 seats where the home games of the local hockey team, the Montreal Canadiens, are played.

❹ Église anglicane Saint-George★

Place du Canada,
1101, rue Stanley
☎ (514) 866 7113
www.st-georges.org

Built between 1869 and 1870,

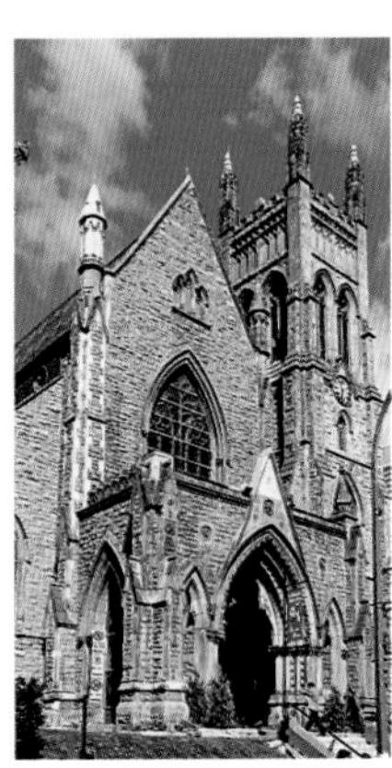

following the plans of William T. Thomas, the Anglican Church of St George, whose sandstone façade is magnificently carved, is a jewel of Neo-Gothic architecture. Its beamed ceiling is one of the largest in the world. The interior is notable for the omnipresent wood and for the many stained-glass windows that lend it a unique ambience.

❺ Planétarium★★

1000, rue Saint-Jacques
☎ (514) 872 4530
Opening times vary, inquire in advance; closed Mon. except in summer.
www.planetarium.montreal.qc.ca
Admission charge.

Opened in 1966, the Planetarium presents, in its Star Theater (topped by a hemispheric 60-ft dome), shows about space sciences and astronomy. These presentations are offered alternately in French and English. Various exhibitions are mounted on particular themes, such as the solar system, meteorites and eclipses.

5

Around Rue Sainte-Catherine

This part of the city is one of the liveliest. Between the countless boutiques on Rue Sainte-Catherine (and underground!), the many office buildings, the university campus and the museums, a rainbow-colored crowd swirls along the streets throughout the day. Join the throng and indulge in a little retail therapy.

❶ Rue Sainte-Catherine★

Between rues Guy and Saint-Denis.

Under constant development since the beginning of the 20th century, Rue Sainte-Catherine, with more than 1,200 shops, is today the country's biggest commercial artery. It also provides access to many subterranean malls.
Here fashion boutiques stand shoulder to shoulder with fast-food joints and nude shows.

❷ Cathédrale Christ Church★

635, rue Sainte-Catherine Ouest
☎ (514) 843 6577
www.montreal.anglican.org/cathedral
Sun.-Fri. 8am-6pm, Sat. 9.30am-6pm.

Modeled on the 14th-century cruciform churches of England, Christ Church Cathedral, built between 1857 and 1859, is a very fine

example of Neo-Gothic architecture. Its simple interior is graced with some fine wood paneling. A shopping mall, "Les Promenades de la Cathédrale," was built directly underneath, giving the builders an opportunity to strengthen the cathedral's foundations!

❸ Musée McCord d'Histoire canadienne★★★

690, rue Sherbrooke Ouest
☎ (514) 398 7100
www.musee-mccord.qc.ca
Tue.-Fri. 10am-6pm, Sat.-Sun. 10am-5pm; in summer Mon. 10am-5pm
Admission charge.

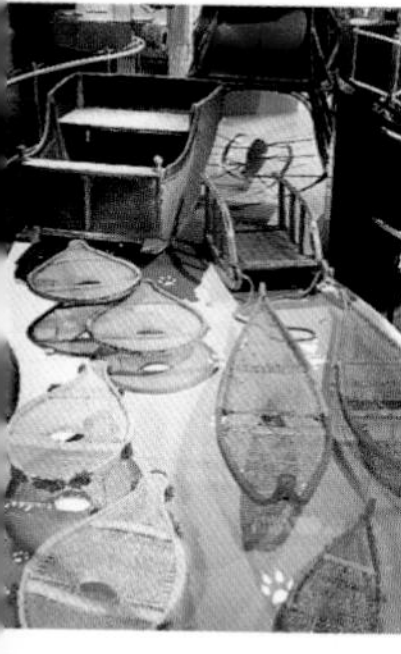

Opened in 1921, this museum bears the name of its founder, David Ross McCord. Wishing to highlight the history and various cultures of his country, this collector covered the length and breadth of Canada in search of representative objects from various eras. In fact, the McCord contains one of the principal historical collections of North America, with artifacts linked to Native American communities and to daily life in the 18th and 19th centuries. The museum holds the Notman Photographic Archives, a priceless iconographic collection dating back to the 1840s.

❹ Caban★★

777, rue Sainte-Catherine Ouest
☎ (514) 844 9300
www.caban.com
Mon.-Fri. 10am-9pm, Sat. 10am-9.30pm, Sun. 11.30am-6pm.

Located in a sublime three-story building, Caban is a boutique devoted to life style. Created by the Club Monaco chain of stores, which belongs nowadays to Ralph Lauren, its design is plain and elegant. Here you will find some original objects for you and your home.

❼ BEN'S DELICATESSEN★

Opened in 1908, this restaurant reminiscent of an old-fashioned cafeteria is a Montreal institution. Here you can eat the famous smoked meat introduced by Jewish immigrants at the beginning of the century. If the decor is too austere, you can always try the same specialty at Schwartz's (see p. 55)!

990, bd de Maisonneuve Ouest
☎ (514) 844 1000
Sun.-Thu. 7.30-2am, Fri.-Sat. 7.30-4am.

❺ McGill University★

805, rue Sherbrooke Ouest
☎ (514) 398 6555
www.mcgill.ca

Founded in 1821, thanks to an endowment by James McGill, a rich fur trader from Scotland, the campus was the first Anglophone university in Canada. Covering an area of 86 acres, it comprises nowadays more than eighty buildings. The main wing, located at the end of the central avenue, is the oldest, and houses the Faculty of Arts. It also contains Moyse Hall, a theater dating from 1926.

❻ Musée Redpath★★

859, rue Sherbrooke Ouest
☎ (514) 398 4086
www.mcgill.ca/redpath
Mon.-Fri. 9am-5pm Sat.-Sun. 1pm-5pm; closed Fri. in summer.
Free admission.

Housed in one of the most attractive McGill University buildings, the Redpath Museum is devoted to natural history. It contains fine collections of paleontology, geology, zoology and ethnology. Several permanent exhibitions are on display, including one on the biological and mineralogical diversity of the province of Quebec.

6

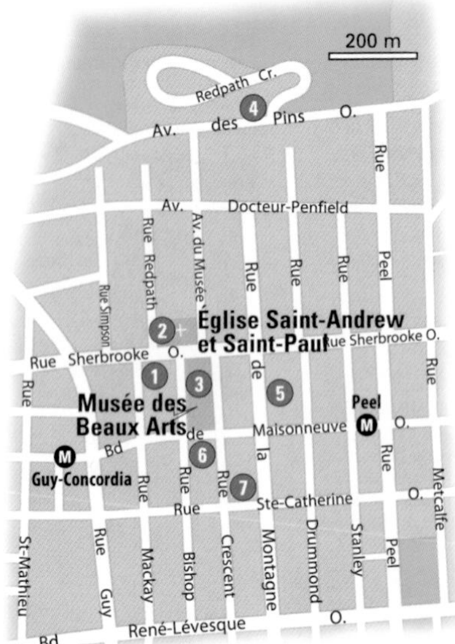

The Golden Square Mile, or museum quarter

In the course of the 19th century, the Anglophone elite, mainly Scottish in origin, installed itself in this area. Since its inhabitants held most of the wealth of Canada in their hands, the area was soon christened "the Golden Square Mile." Even today its prestige is undiminished, thanks to the period residences on Avenue des Pins, as well as its numerous art galleries and stylish boutiques, not to mention the unmissable Musée des Beaux-Arts.

❶ Guilde canadienne des métiers d'art★★

1460, rue Sherbrooke Ouest
☎ (514) 849 6091
www.canadianguild.com
Tue.-Fri. 10am-6pm, Sat. 10am-5pm.

The Canadian Guild of Craft, established in 1906, is a not-for-profit organization whose aim is to conserve, foster and promote the crafts and fine arts of Canada. It exhibits and puts on sale single works or limited series of Inuit art (from 1900 to the present day), Native American art and contemporary art, along with, among other items, a fine collection of jewelry and ceramics.

❷ Eglise Saint-Andrew and Saint-Paul★

Intersection of rue Sherbrooke Ouest and rue Redpath
☎ (514) 842 3431
www.standrewstpaul.com

This imposing Presbyterian church, built in 1932, is one of

❼ OGILVY★

A veritable institution, the origin of the Ogilvy couturier business dates back to 1866. Despite the rearrangement of this large shop into several independent boutiques, the interior of the building has kept part of its decor as well as the Tudor Hall located on the fifth floor. A bagpiper plays every day at noon.

1307, rue Sainte-Catherine Ouest
☎ (514) 842 7711
www.ogilvycanada.com
Mon.-Wed. 10am-6pm, Thu.-Fri. 10am-9pm, Sat. 10am-5pm, Sun. 12-5pm.

ıe most important ıstitutions of the Scottish ɔmmunity. Its stone interior, ıedieval in inspiration, has ıagnificent commemorative ɪained-glass windows. Right eside the building, a little arden has been laid out.

❸ Musée des ɜeaux-Arts★★★

379, and 1380, rue ɜherbrooke Ouest
ɜ (514) 285 2000
ɿww.mbam.qc.ca
ue.-Sun. 11am-5pm, ntil 9pm Wed., open ɿon. in summer. ɿdmission charge for emporary exhibitions only.
ɜee Don't Miss p. 78.

'ounded in 1860, the Museum ɜ the oldest in Quebec, and ɿolds a rich and varied ollection, bringing together very art form from antiquity ɔ the present day. It extends ɿver two buildings, the Michal ɿnd Renata Horstein Pavilion (whose design recalls ancient Rome) and the Jean-Noël Desmarais Pavilion, opened in 1991 and displaying a great part of the collection as well as mounting some interesting temporary exhibitions.

❹ Avenue des Pins Ouest★★

Between rue McTavish and rue Redpath.

Avenue des Pins is one of the rare streets of the quarter with sumptuous residences, built between 1850 and 1930, reflecting the wealth of the Canadian elite of the period. Among them is Ravenscrag (no. 1025), resembling a castle with its more than 60 rooms, or, in contrasting styles, the house of Henry V. Meredith (no. 1110) and that of Clarence-de-Sola (no. 1374).

❺ Nadya Toto★★

2057, rue de la Montagne
☎ (514) 350 9090
www.nadyatoto.com
Mon.-Wed. and Sat. 10am-5pm, Thu.-Fri. 10am-7pm.

Italian by birth, this designer is one of the big names in Quebec fashion. In the midst of a magnificent boutique (whose design won her the Montreal Commerce Design first prize in 1998), Nadya Toto dresses women in only the best materials. An elegant source of exquisite clothing.

❻ Newtown★★

1476, rue Crescent
☎ (514) 284 6555
www.newtown.ca
Lounge: Mon.-Thu. 11.30am-2am, Fri.-Sun. 11.30am-3am
Restaurant: Sun.-Thu. 5.30pm-10pm, Fri.-Sat. 5.30pm-10.30pm.

Created by the Formula 1 racing driver Jacques Villeneuve, Newtown is a splendid four-story complex, inserted behind a Victorian façade. Eat and drink at any hour in the lounge, restaurant, night club or roof terrace. The lounge has some delicious and inexpensive dishes on offer.

7

From Place des Arts to the Chinese quarter

Performances of dance, theater, music, opera and ballet are features of this area, as well as exhibitions of contemporary art. It's a place pulsating with life, and where creativity is highly regarded. A little further south, the Chinese quarter, full of colors and aromas, continues the show.

❶ Musée d'Art contemporain★★★

185, rue Sainte-Catherine Ouest
☎ (514) 847 6226
www.macm.org
Tue.-Sun. 11am-6pm (until 9pm Wed.)
Admission charge except Wed. from 6pm.
See Don't Miss p. 77.

The only Canadian institution devoted exclusively to contemporary art, this museum offers a rich and varied program of Québécois, Canadian and international artists. The building has eight rooms, a shop, a restaurant and a sculpture garden. The

permanent collection contains almost 6,000 works from several disciplines: painting, drawing, engraving, sculpture, photography, installation and video.

❷ Place des Arts★

175, rue Sainte-Catherine Ouest
☎ (514) 842 2112
www.pda.qc.ca

A cultural complex opened in 1963 (modeled on the Lincoln Center in New York), Place des Arts groups together five theaters and concert halls. In the middle, the largest, Salle Wilfrid-Pelletier, stages performances by the Montreal Symphony Orchestra, the Montreal Opera and Les Grands Ballets Canadiens. To the right the theater complex includes Théâtre Maisonneuve, Théâtre

Jean-Duceppe and the Studio Theatre. Lastly, beneath the Museum of Contemporary Art is the Cinquième Salle (Fifth Room), a multipurpose space adaptable to performances of music, dance or theater.

❸ Complexe Desjardins★

150, rue Sainte-Catherine Ouest
☎ (514) 845 4636
www.complexedesjardins.com; Mon.-Wed. 9.30am-6pm, Thu.-Fri. 9.30am-9pm, Sat. 9.30am-5pm, Sun. noon-5pm.

Opened in 1976, this complex includes offices, the headquarters of la Fédération des caisses populaires Desjardins (community-based financial institutions), a hotel and a total of 110 shops and restaurants. In the heart of the complex is Grande-Place, with its glorious fountain. This is a popular meeting point where performances, such as the "little school of jazz" during the Montreal Jazz Festival, take place frequently.

❹ Église de Gesù, Centre de Créativité★★

1202, rue de Bleury
☎ (514) 866 2305
www.gesu.net

Built in 1865 as a chapel for St Mary's College, a Jesuit institution since demolished, Église de Gesù is now a creativity center dedicated to the visual, literary and dramatic arts. The interior contains some fine wood paneling from the era of its construction, and pictures of saints side-by-side with contemporary art works. Beneath the chapel, a room with more than 400 seats hosts numerous performances.

❺ Chinese quarter★

Between bd René-Lévesque and av Viger to the south and rues Jeanne-Mance and Saint-Dominique to the west.

Evolved in the second half of the 19th century, as a consequence of several waves of immigration, the Chinese quarter is a little area of exoticism in the heart of Montreal. Marked by four splendid gateways, replicas of originals in imperial China, a plethora of characteristic shops, stalls and restaurants is contained within. Among the distinctive sights are the calligraphy stand (intersection of rues Clark and de la Gauchetière), the Catholic Chinese Mission (205, rue de la Gauchetière Ouest) and the pagodas on the roof of the Holiday Inn (99, av Viger).

❻ DRAGON'S BEARD CANDY★★

A tiny counter offers a sweet specialty that you won't find anywhere else: Dragon's Beard candy. These are small sweetmeats, hard to describe, made from sugar, groundnuts, sesame seeds, coconut and chocolate. They get their name from their stringy, beard-like appearance ($3 for a box of six).

52, rue de la Gauchetière Ouest.

8

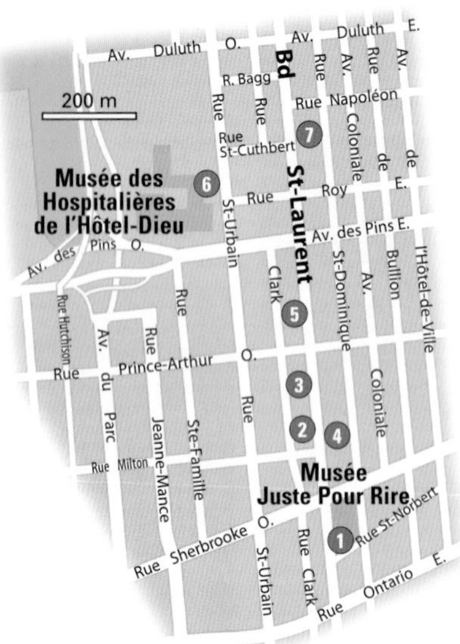

"Main,"
cradle of Montreal

Dividing the east of the city from the west, Boulevard Saint-Laurent, called "Main" (or "Main Street"), is at the core of Montreal's history. It has welcomed many waves of immigration, traces of which remain in places like the famous Schwartz's. While the Portuguese, Greek and Italian neighborhoods still exist, this long arterial road plays host today to a throng of stylish bars, boutiques and restaurants.

❶ Musée Juste Pour Rire★

2111, bd Saint-Laurent
☎ (514) 845 4000
www.hahaha.com
Admission charge
Groups of 15 people or more must make an advance reservation.

Following the tremendous success of the Just For Laughs Festival, its founder Gilbert Rozon decided, in 1993, to create a space entirely devoted to the distinctive contribution made to cultural life by laughter and humor. The museum now displays a small collection of artifacts dating from the early days of cinema comedy, at the start of the 20th century, up to the present day, and shows excerpts from the best movies (two and a half hours).

❷ M0851★★

3526, bd Saint-Laurent
☎ (514) 849 9759
www.m0851.com
Mon.-Wed. and Sat. 10am-6pm, Thu.-Fri. 10am-9pm, Sun. noon-5pm.

Formerly operating under the name of Rugb North America, since 1987 this Montreal firm ha been making garments and accessories in high-quality leather. Its collection c luggage and purses is out of his world. From the smallest wallet to the largest traveling bag, the colors are exceptional and the finishing impeccable.

❸ Ex-Centris★

3536, bd Saint-Laurent
☎ (514) 847 2206
www.ex-centris.com

Founded in 1999 by Daniel Langlois, the famous creator of Softimage software (see p. 27), Ex-Centris is an avant-garde center fostering independent movie-making and films using the latest digital technology. The complex plays host to different movie festivals, including Mutek (see p. 21), photography exhibitions and acoustic concerts. On the first floor, Café Méliès serves a succulent menu.

❹ Lola & Emily★

3475, bd Saint-Laurent
☎ (514) 288 7598
www.lolaandemily.com
Sat.-Wed. noon-6pm,
Thu.-Fri. noon-9pm.

To go shopping as if you were visiting a friend is the idea behind Lola & Emily: a marvelous loft, furnished like an apartment, where everything is for sale, from the sofa to the underwear! The clothes are arranged in beautiful second-hand closets and the cosmetics are laid out on shelves. It all goes to make an incredibly laid back atmosphere. You'll almost think you're in your own home.

❺ Space FB★

3632, bd Saint-Laurent
☎ (514) 282 1991
www.spacefb.com
Mon.-Fri. 11am-9pm,
Sat. 11am-midnight,
Sun. noon-9pm.

François Beauregard could be called the sweater specialist! This Québécois designer only uses jersey cloth in producing his clothes in a range of soft and varied colors. One word of warning: They seem to have been made for those with perfect figures!

❻ Musée des Hospitalières de l'Hôtel-Dieu★★

201, av des Pins Ouest
☎ (514) 849 2919; www.museedeshospitalieres.qc.ca
Mid-Jun. to mid-Oct., Tue.-Fri. 10am-5pm, Sat.-Sun. 1pm-5pm; mid-Oct to mid-Jun,: Wed.-Sun. 1pm-5pm
Admission charge.

Established in a former missionary residence, beside the Hôtel-Dieu hospital (not far from Boulevard Saint-Laurent), the museum recounts the history of the founding of Montreal through the story of the Hospitallers of St Joseph. Thanks to a rich permanent collection of several thousand objects, you will learn about the development of early medicine and nursing care in recent centuries.

❼ SCHWARTZ'S★★

It was in 1927 that Ruben Schwartz, of Rumanian Jewish descent, opened this delicatessen, the first of its type in Canada. The distinctive flavor of its smoked meat soon made it a legend. Even today the meat is still prepared each day according to the original recipe. Whether in a sandwich or simply sliced, Schwartz's fare will provide you with an eating experience that is quintessential Montreal.

3895, bd Saint-Laurent
☎ (514) 842 4813
www.schwartzsdeli.com
Sun.-Thu. 8am-12.30am,
Fri. 8am-1.30am,
Sat. 8am-2.30am.

9

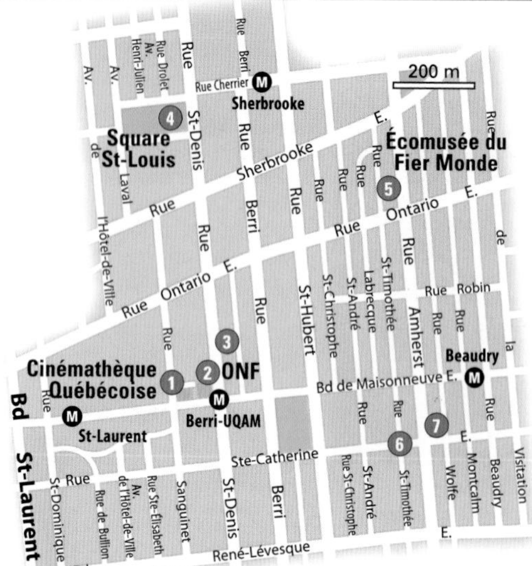

From the Latin Quarter to the Village

The former home of the French-speaking bourgeoisie, the Latin Quarter remains a place strongly Gallic in its culture, symbolized by the University of Quebec at Montreal (UQAM), the Grande Bibliothèque and numerous cinemas and theaters. Rue Saint-Denis, its main artery, is in perpetual motion, with its wealth of boutiques and restaurants. For a really boisterous evening, you might venture into Montreal's Gay Village, along Rue Sainte-Catherine.

❶ Cinémathèque québécoise*

335, bd de Maisonneuve Est
☎ (514) 842 9763
www.cinematheque.qc.ca
Exhibitions:
Tue.-Fri. noon-9pm,
Sat.-Sun. 5-9pm;
Multimedia library:
Tue.-Fri. 1-8pm
Admission charge except for exhibitions.

Established in 1963 by a group of passionate movie-lovers, the Quebec Cinémathèque defined itself as a museum of the moving image. Its mission was to conserve and document the heritage of cinema and television. It consists of several rooms for projections and exhibitions, a médiathèque (multimedia library), a shop and a delightful café with a splendid terrace.

❼ CABARET MADO★

A place well known among Village nighthawks, the Cabaret Mado and its troupe of drag queens present irreverent performances seasoned with caustic humor. In a flashy setting amid a warm ambience, Mado and friends improvise with *éclat*. For those eager to exercise their vocal cords, Monday evenings are usually given over to karaoke.

1115, rue Sainte-Catherine Est
☎ (514) 525 7566
www.mado.qc.ca
Mon.-Sun. 11-3am.

❷ Ciné-Robothèque★★

1564, rue Saint-Denis
☎ (514) 496 6887
www.onf.ca/cinerobotheque
Tue.-Sun. noon-9pm
Admission charge.

The CinéRobothèque belongs to the NFB (National Film Board of Canada), a public organization that produces and distributes audiovisual works to help aquaint people with Canada. It possesses more than twenty viewing stations, where you can see in excess of 4,500 films in French and 6,200 in English. This institution also has two projection rooms and offers workshops on various themes.

❸ Brûlerie Saint-Denis★

1587, rue Saint-Denis
☎ (514) 286 9159
3967, rue Saint-Denis
☎ (514) 286-9158
Mon.-Thu. 8am-11pm, Fri.-Sat. 8am-midnight, Sun. 9am-11pm.

Since 1985, this Montreal coffee-roasters has offered a wide selection of coffee. From the rich, scented coffee beans of Indonesia to subtle blends like Mocca-Java and the surprising aromatic flavor of hazelnut vanilla, everything is delectable.

❹ Square Saint-Louis★★

Once the water reservoir of Old Montreal and now fringed by magnificent Victorian dwellings built between 1890 and 1900, the Square was the main residential area for the French bourgeoisie. Several artists, such as the poet Émile Nelligan and the singer Pauline Julien, moved into the area. West of the Square, Rue Prince-Arthur, was the rallying

point for free thinkers in the 1960s.

❺ Écomusée du Fier Monde★★

2050, rue Amherst
☎ (514) 528 8444
www.ecomusee.qc.ca
Wed. 11am-8pm, Thu.-Fri. 9.30am-4pm, Sat.-Sun. 10.30am-5pm
Admission charge.

Established in a former art deco public baths in this industrial, working-class area of Montreal, this museum ("of the Proud World") paints a broad picture of the daily life of laborers and their families. Temporary exhibitions focus on particular aspects of the heritage of the area.

❻ Le Village★

Rue Sainte-Catherine Est, between rues Saint-Hubert and Papineau.

The Village is one of the most important centers of gay life in the world. The gay community settled here in the 1980s, a time when this old industrial area was falling into decay. Since then, a multitude of shops, bars and restaurants has brought the quarter back to life, and it is especially renowned for its raucous nightlife.

10

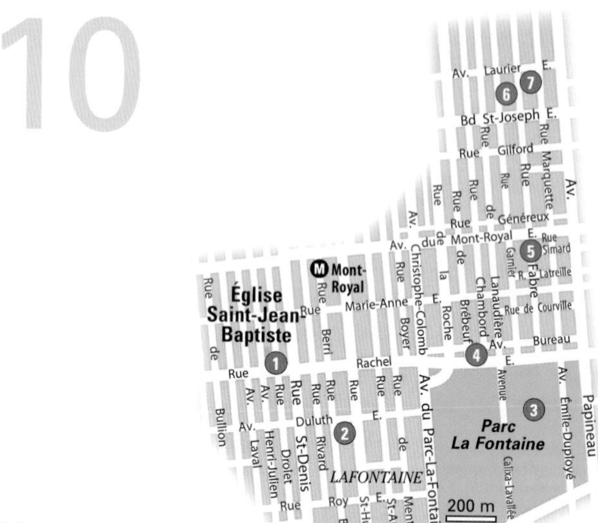

Plateau Mont-Royal

Truly a village within the city, the Plateau is a residential district whose two- and three-storied houses, graced with outside stairways, make an essential contribution to the distinctive charm of Montreal.The proximity of Mont-Royal and the attractiveness of Parc La Fontaine make this a favorite spot for families, sports lovers and outdoor enthusiasts.

❶ Église Saint-Jean-Baptiste★

309, rue Rachel Est
☎ (514) 842 9811.

Dating from 1875, the Church of St John the Baptist, twice the victim of fire, was rebuilt in 1912 after the design of Casimir Saint-Jean. Its austere façade conceals a glorious interior, Neo-Baroque in inspiration and endowed with rich architectural ornamentation in molded plaster, original chandeliers and an organ with the Casavant & Brothers trademark. Frequent concerts are given here, and guided tours are available during summer.

❷ Au Pied de Cochon★★

536, rue Duluth Est
☎ (514) 281 1114
www.aupieddecochon.ca
Tue.-Sun. 5pm-midnight.

An essential place for sampling the flavors of North America. It caters particularly to carnivores, but fish-lovers will succumb to the charms of mouth-watering lobster. For those with large appetites, *côte de cochon heureux* (happy pork chop), *poutine au foie gras* and *côtes levées de cerf* (boned venison chops) should do the job! In view of the popularity of this restaurant, it's best to reserve in advance.

❸ Parc La Fontaine★★

The third largest park in Montreal, Parc La Fontaine was laid out on the grounds of the former Logan farm. With an area of 100 acres, it possesses two ponds (separated by a

waterfall) that welcome pedal-boaters in summer and ice-skaters in winter, as well as sports areas and the Théâtre de Verdure, where you can see open-air shows and concerts in the summer season.

❹ La Maison des Cyclistes★

1251, rue Rachel Est
☎ (514) 521 8356
www.velo.qc.ca
Mon.-Fri. 8.30am-6pm, Sat.-Sun. 9am-6pm.

Perfectly located at the crossroads of two cycling tracks, opposite Parc La Fontaine, La Maison des Cyclistes is considered the cycling cultural center of Quebec. It contains a shop selling maps, guides and accessories for cyclists, as well as a travel agency specializing in tours by bicycle. A little café, with a terrace opening onto the park, offers agreeable light meals.

❺ Rue Fabre★★

Between rue Rachel and av Laurier

Rue Fabre is a good example of typical Plateau architecture. Constructed between 1900 and 1930, its houses of two or three stories, called duplex or triplex, are divided into several apartments accessible by exterior stairways. The clash of colors, the prevalence of

balconies, the uniqueness of the stairways and the beauty of its flowery terraces make this a quarter full of character.

❻ Maison Cakao★

5090, rue Fabre
☎ (514) 598 2462
Tue.-Wed. 10am-6pm, Thu.-Fri. 10am-8pm, Sat. 10am-5pm, Sun. noon-5pm; closed Jul. 15-30.

This tiny shop expresses perfectly the soul of the area. Inside you can sample delicious warm chocolate, prepared with traditional skill, and some surprising little tidbits. For hungrier customers, the home-made cake (chocolate, of course) is dispensed in portions generous enough to satisfy the emptiest stomach. A small haven of self-indulgence!

❼ GAIA, POTTERY WORKSHOP-BOUTIQUE★★

Catherine Auriol and Marko Savard wanted to create a place of creativity, work and production based on their passion: pottery. Next to their workshop, where you can see the artists at their labors, the shop displays the products of twenty or so Québécois artisans, each imbued with the individual stamp of their creator: Functional objects, such as plates, teapots and cups, sit cheek by jowl with purely decorative pieces. You'll be pleasantly astonished by the individual artistry of these works.

1590, rue Laurier Est
☎ (514) 598 5444
www.gaiaceramique.com
Tue., Wed. and Sat. 10am-5pm, Thu.-Fri. 10am-7pm.

11

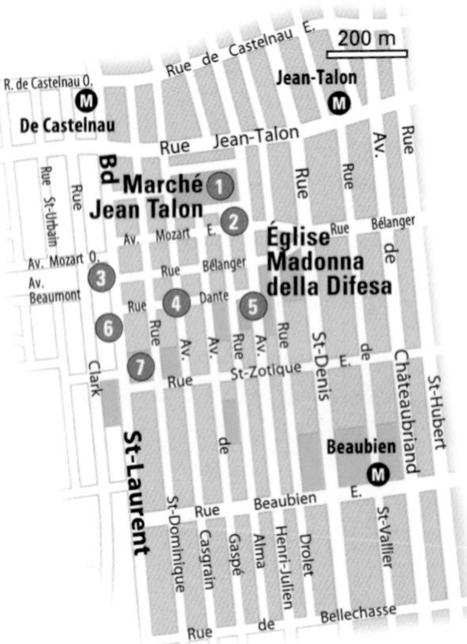

Little Italy

Arriving at the end of the 19th century, then in another wave after the Second World War, the Italians, mainly from Sicily and southern Italy, are the most important ethnic community in Montreal. Even if this area is not inhabited or frequented by them alone, there reigns here an atmosphere typically Mediterranean, with cafés, trattorias and restaurants overflowing the sidewalks around Boulevard Saint-Laurent.

❶ Marché Jean-Talon★★

7075, av Casgrain
☎ (514) 277 1588
Mon.-Sun. from 8am.

Opened in 1934, Jean Talon Market is one of the city's three big public markets. In its midst, the producers and sellers of fruit, flowers and vegetables congregate. Don't be shy about tasting the produce that they graciously offer you; its tastiness will surprise you. All around are stalls specializing in particular foods, as well as convenient cafés of a multicultural character.

❷ Marché des Saveurs du Québec★★

280, place du Marché du Nord
☎ (514) 271 3811
Sat.-Wed. 9am-6pm, Thu.-Fri. 9am-8pm.

This "market of the flavors of Quebec" should be on the itinerary of every visitor to Montreal. Here you will find all the local produce you may not find elsewhere: products of the maple tree (butter, conserve, relish, tea), game pâtés, rose jellies, fruit ketchup, flavored honey, marinated *têtes de violons*, Quebec cheeses and *coeurs de quenouilles* (cat-tail hearts). The hardest choice will be what to leave behind.

3 Milano★

862, bd Saint-Laurent
☎ (514) 273 8558
Mon.-Wed. 8am-6.pm,
'hu.-Fri. 8am-9pm, Sat.-Sun.
am-5pm.

'his huge Italian supermarket, n which not only the Italian ommunity but the whole of Aontreal descends in search of asta and Mediterranean roduce, has become a real nstitution. The home-made *harcuterie* (cooked meat), esh pastries, imported heeses, ready-made dishes nd the numerous aisles filled vith coffee, olive oil and other oodstuffs, all bring the uthentic flavor of Italy to this orner of the city.

4 Rue Dante★

Rue Dante contains several key ddresses in Little Italy. First of ll, you'll find a genuine talian bakery at Alati-Caserta (no. 277), known for its tasty anola and dry biscuits. A little arther, at no. 189, the Napoletana pizzeria – an unpretentious restaurant with n unprepossessing ppearance – is celebrated for ts succulent pizzas on thin or rusty bases. It is not uthorized to sell alcohol, but you can bring your own wine. Lastly, on the corner of Rue Saint-Dominique, an immense hardware store displays every kitchen utensil you ever dreamed of – and more.

5 Église Madonna della Difesa★

6810, av Henri-Julien
Sunday Mass: 8.30am and 11am in Italian, 10am in French.

This church was built in 1919, following the plans of the architect R. Montbirant and the designs of the painter, master glazier and decorator Guido Nincheri. The latter also created the frescoes in the interior. One of these, located above the high altar, depicts Mussolini on his horse. This has been a bone of contention for some time!

6 Café Italia★

6840, bd Saint-Laurent
☎ (514) 495 0059
Mon.-Sun. 6am-11pm.

It's not for its rudimentary décor and nondescript appearance that the Café Italia is appreciated, but for its authentic Italian atmosphere (soccer games on the television), its excellent sandwiches and, especially, its delicious cappuccino, considered by some to be the best in town. Ice-cream lovers should continue a little farther, to Pile ou Glace (no. 7084).

7 MIMI & COCO★★

It was in 1993 that Vincenzo Cavallo created this brand of T-shirts in Montreal. The kinds of cotton used, including the famous Scottish thread, are of high quality and the choice of color is impressive. The "Pointelle" collection for women, with its lace trimmings and its "lingerie" look, is appreciated for its refinement. This business has turned out to be a great success, and well deserves its place in Little Italy.

6717, bd Saint-Laurent
☎ (514) 274 6262
www.mimicoco.com
Mon.-Wed. 11am-6pm, Thu.-Fri. 11am-8pm, Sat. 11am-5pm, Sun. noon-5pm.

12

Outremont, a history in green

It's because of its location on the other side of "la Montagne" (the Mountain) that this region has been christened "outre mont" (beyond the mountain). This residential area offers the opportunity for a peaceful walk between natural scenery and the beautiful bourgeois residences on Maplewood, Bloomfield and Outremont Avenues. In the heart of the Montreal Hassidic Jewish community, you can sample genuine bagels at Fairmount or Saint-Viateur (see p. 119).

❶ Maplewood Avenue★★

Also called "Avenue of Power," Maplewood Avenue is bordered by luxurious houses of varying architecture. Located on the heights of Outremont, on the northeast side of "la Montagne" ("the Mountain" – affectionat nickname for Parc du Mont-Royal), this splendid avenue, with the look of a bourgeois landscape, is well worth a sho stroll. Among its curiosities ar the houses at nos. 47 and 49, dating from 1906 (the oldest i the street), no. 77 with its colonial style, and no. 118, embellished by a little stream.

❷ Parc Beaubien and Parc Outremont★

As well as magnificent leafy streets, the Outremont area boasts many green spaces. Th parks of Beaubien and Outremont are greatly cherished by the residents. Th former, very hilly, is graced by a fine pond and picnic tables, while the latter enjoys a lovely location, expansive play areas and a ravishing ornamental

pond adorned with a fountain inspired by the groups of children at the Château of Versailles.

❸ Kabane★

1061, av Bernard Ouest
☎ (514) 490 1061
Mon.-Wed. 10am-6pm,
Thu.-Fri. 10am-8pm,
Sat. 10am-5pm.

This shop sells marvelous little lavender-scented silk squares created by Estelle Billot, waxed hand-painted canvas bags from Mexico, and lots of other original items to take home as presents.

❹ L'Arterie★★

176, av Bernard Ouest
☎ (514) 273 3933
Tue.-Sun. noon-6pm.

Behind its air of a happy-go-lucky secondhand shambles, this colorful shop is shared and managed by several artisans. Here you won't find typical Québecois handicrafts, but original creations and outrageous clothes and accessories of all sorts, such as the dolls of Dana De Kuyper, real little monsters but irresistible. Not to be missed.

❺ Milos★★

5357, av du Parc
☎ (514) 272 3522
www.milos.ca
Mon.-Fri. 12-3pm,
Mon.-Sun. 5.30-11.30pm.

Opened by Costas Spiliadis in 1980, Milos is nothing like other Greek restaurants. Here the décor is elegant and undemonstrative; the olive oil, extremely tasty, is home-made, and the fish is cooked on charcoal. The menu offers simple but refined dishes, incorporating a large selection of salads and main courses. For dessert, the yoghurt with honey is unbeatable. Considered one of the best restaurants in town, a visit here could make your day.

❻ La Croissanterie Figaro★

5200, rue Hutchinson
☎ (514) 278 6567
Every day 7am-1am.

A charming café in the heart of a residential area.
The old chandeliers, the wood paneling and the marble tables give a Belle Époque flavor to this cozy spot frequented by local residents and romantic souls from elsewhere. A little terrace adds to the delight of a sunny day. Here you can eat light meals, especially the delicious whole-wheat croissants, cinnamon bread, carrot muffins. Delicious!

❼ FAIRMOUNT BAGEL★★

This family bakery, founded in 1919, carries on the tradition of the genuine bagel, shaped by hand and cooked in a wood stove. At Fairmount Bagel you can eat specialties that you won't find elsewhere, like bagels with black rye, cornflower, buckwheat, chocolate, muesli, pesto and even dried tomatoes. A treat!

74, rue Fairmount Ouest
☎ (514) 272 0667
www.fairmountbagel.com
Every day 24 hours.

13

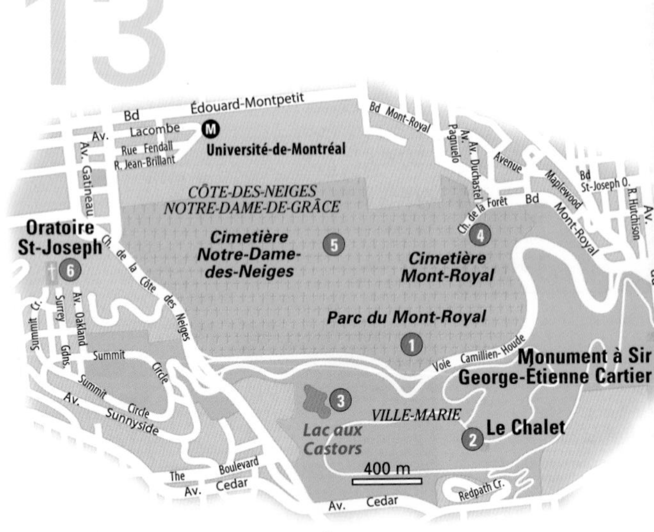

Mont-Royal
and its environs

Affectionately nicknamed "la Montagne," Parc du Mont-Royal, reaching a height of 750ft, is the highest point in Montreal. The "lungs" of the city, this is the spot to come with family or friends to enjoy the fresh air or practice sports: cycling, hiking, as well as skiing and ice-skating in winter. This unique location is a jewel whose summit offers one of the best views over the city.

❶ Parc du Mont-Royal★★★

☎ (514) 843 8240
www.lemontroyal.qc.ca
See Don't Miss p. 81.

In the middle of the 19th century, the city bought some land on "la Montagne" (the Mountain) for the creation of a large public park. Frederick Law Olmsted, the famous designer of Central Park in New York, drew up the plans. Opened in 1876, Mont-Royal Park covers more than 250 acres. It comprises numerous footpaths, several cycle tracks and a collection of 700 plant species. The large metal cross erected on the summit of the east side was raised to the memory of Maisonneuve, Montreal's founder, who had himself raised a monument to thank the Virgin for having saved the city from a flood.

❷ Chalet du Parc du Mont-Royal★★

Summit of Mont-Royal
☎ (514) 872 3911
Mon.-Sun. 8.30am-9pm.

Built in 1932 by Aristide Beaugrand-Champagne, the Chalet de la Montagne (Mountain Chalet) was a highly prized venue, where

ɔig-band orchestras performed n the 1940s. The large hall is ɪdorned with pictures tracing the ɪistory of Montreal, painted by eading artists (one of whom was Marc-Aurèle Fortin). Opposite he chalet, the Kondiaronk scenic lookout offers an unrestricted view over the city.

3 Lac aux Castors★

Along chemin Remembrance.

Laid out in the middle of the 19th century, the lac aux Castors (Beaver Lake) is small but charming. Surrounded by large lawns and a sculpture garden, it's a perfect picnic spot where you can laze in the summer sun. In winter, the lake is transformed into a skating rink.

4 Cimetière Mont-Royal★★

Chemin Camillien-Houde or chemin de la Forêt
☎ (514) 279 7358
www.mountroyalcem.com

Established in 1853 on former agricultural land, Cimetière Mont-Royal is one of the most beautiful garden cemeteries in North America. Arranged in terraces, it follows the topography of the site. It's said to support 145 species of birds, and nature here is luxuriant. Many well-known people are laid to rest here, including John Molson, founder of the famous Molson's Brewery.

5 Cimetière Notre-Dame-des-Neiges★★

4601, chemin de la Côte-des-Neiges
☎ (514) 343 6111
www.cimetierenddn.org

This Catholic cemetery, laid out in 1854, is one of the largest in Canada. More than 870,000 people are buried here. It contains some magnificent religious structures, including the impressive St Peter and St Paul Mausoleum and the lovely little Resurrection Chapel. Among the celebrities buried here are Jean Drapeau, former mayor of Montreal, and the poet Émile Nelligan.

6 Oratoire Saint-Joseph★★★

3800, chemin Queen-Mary
☎ (514) 733 8211
www.saint-joseph.org
Mon.-Sun. 6am-10pm
See Don't Miss p. 76

This majestic sanctuary is one of the most visited pilgrimage sites in the world. The construction of the first chapel dates back to 1904, at the instigation of Brother André, a porter at Notre Dame College (located opposite).
The oratory, forming a religious complex, includes a votive chapel, a crypt, a museum, a primitive chapel, a spectacular basilica and a Way of the Cross located in a neighboring garden.

THE TAM-TAMS

On summer Sunday afternoons, at the foot of the monument dedicated to George-Etienne Cartier (on Avenue du Parc), a crowd gathers to participate in unison in a communal ritual called "the tam-tams." Amateur drummers play for hours on end, accompanying the spontaneous improvisations of any members of the public seized by the urge to dance. An unforgettable summer moment.

14

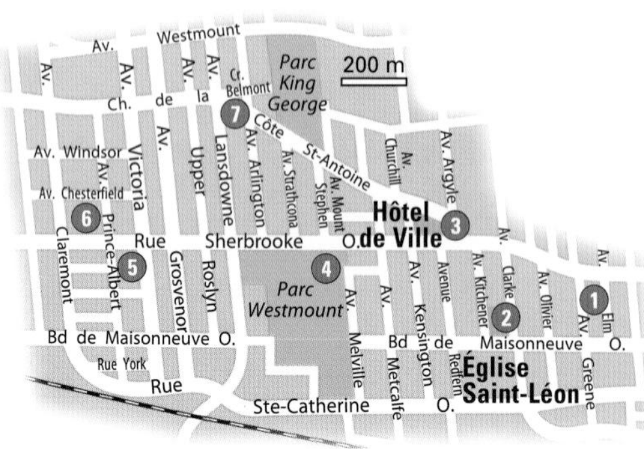

Westmount, an independent suburb

Stronghold of the English-speaking bourgeoisie and a symbol of social success, Westmount is a haven of peace bordered by magnificent buildings, beginning with the City Hall and its air of a haunted castle. Absorbed officially as a district of Montreal some years ago, its residents then voted hugely in favor of a return to their independence. This area is highly coveted, and fiercely contested!

❶ La Cache★

1353, av Greene
☎ (514) 935 4361
Mon.-Wed. 9.30am-6pm, Thu.-Fri. 9.30am-7pm, Sat. 9.30am-5pm, Sun. noon-5pm.

The bright and flowery fabrics created by April Cornell appear nowadays in a hundred shops across America. This delightful three-story boutique offers a range of brightly colored garments with matching accessories.

There is also a section aimed specifically at young girls, likely to prove the financial ruin of many a mother!

❷ Église Saint-Léon★★

4311, bd de Maisonneuve O.
Mon.-Fri. 9am-noon and 1.30-6pm.

Église Saint-Léon is the church for the only French-speaking Catholic parish in Westmount. The Neo-Romanesque façade conceals beautifully decorated interior created between 1928 and 1944 by Guido Nincheri. This Canadian artist, of Italian origin, was honored by the Vatican as one of the greatest religious artists in the world. The radiant colors of the frescoes were achieved by the traditional egg-tempera technique.

❼ CHEMIN DE LA CÔTE-SAINT-ANTOINE★★

Adapted in 1684 by the Sulpician order from the remains of a Native American trail, Chemin de la Côte-Saint-Antoine leads to the oldest dwellings in Westmount, of which the most venerable, Maison Hurtubise, is located at no. 563. Built in 1688 by Pierre Hurtubise, it was also nicknamed La Haute Folie (The Height of Folly), because its out-of-the-way location rendered it vulnerable to attack by Amerindians. Along the length of the road, magnificent residences look down on you. An architectural feast!

❸ Hôtel de Ville★

4333, rue Sherbrooke Ouest.

At first sight, you might take this for a castle, or the property of someone stupendously rich, but this monument festooned with ivy is in fact the City Hall. The magnificent building, in Neo-Tudor style, is the work of the architect Robert Findley, who provided Westmount with some of its other public buildings.

❹ Parc Westmount★

Laid out in 1895 on marshy terrain, Westmount Park can boast, in addition to several sports areas and a small ornamental pond, several architectural curiosities, such as Victoria Hall (in the same style as the City Hall) and the gorgeous municipal library. The latter, built in 1899 in a Neo-Romaneque style, was one of the first public libraries in Quebec. Next to it is a conservatory from the same epoch, where temporary exhibitions are organized.

❺ Bead Emporium★★

368, av Victoria
☎ (514) 486 6425
Mon.-Fri. 10am-6pm (Thu. until 7pm), Sat. 10am-5pm.

Lovers of do-it-yourself jewelry will spend hours in this shop with its beads from around the world which you can fashion into items of your choice. The possibilities are endless: cylindrical Greek pots, clay pearls, brooches, mother-of pearl, painted wood figurines, religious medallions, a feathery fan, or sequins you can sew onto your purse, shoes or dress. For those whose fingers are not so deft, a selection of handmade jewelry is conveniently on sale.

❻ Ben & Tournesol★

4915, rue Sherbrooke Ouest
☎ (514) 481 5050
Mon.-Wed. 10am-6pm, Thu.-Fri. 10am-9pm, Sat. 10am-5pm, Sun. noon-5pm.

An unusual shop chockful of bright ideas for presents! There are many modern items for kitchen or bathroom, as well as shelves stuffed with zany objects and idiosyncratic accessories. From enormous "Groovy Girl" dolls, to ultra-cool Matt & Nat purses and collars for mad dogs, there's something for the whole family, and to suit every taste!

15

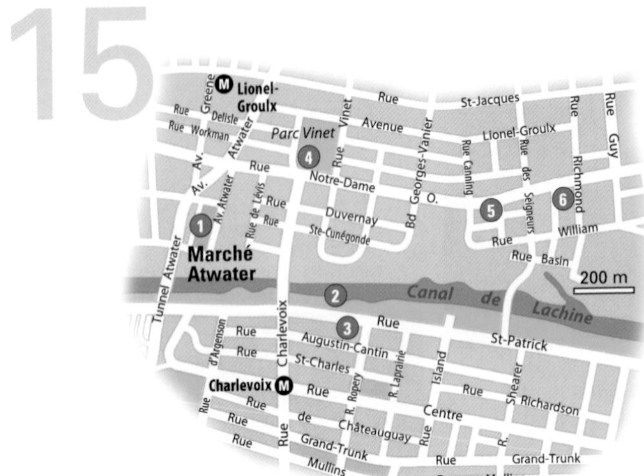

Little Burgundy and the banks of Lachine Canal

Little Burgundy (once a vineyard) is a former working-class quarter. The proximity of the canal gives it a surprisingly rural air. People come here to stroll by the canal, do their shopping or search for antiques on Rue Notre-Dame. You get the pleasant impression that you have left the city behind, even though its center is only a stone's throw away.

❶ Marché Atwater★

138, av Atwater
☎ (514) 937 7754
Mon.-Wed. 8am-6pm,
Thu. 8am-8pm,
Fri. 8am-9pm,
Sat.-Sun. 8am-5pm.

Built in 1933 in art deco style, and perfectly located next the Lachine Canal, this lively market draws crowds of Montrealers. Meat, cheese and fish shops are located in the interior (for reasons of hygiene, a law forbids them from selling their produce outside), along with spice merchants and an irresistible bakery. On the outside, fruits and vegetables vie for elbow-room with a profusion of flowers. The sights and scents will make your head spin!

❷ Canal de Lachine★★

Cruise information:
☎ (514) 846 0428
www.croisierecanaldelachine.ca

Dug between 1821 and 1825, enlarged between 1840 and 1870, the Lachine Canal, linking the Atlantic Ocean to the Great Lakes, was then the longest internal navigational passage in the world. However, the opening of the St Lawrence Seaway, in 1959, brought about its inevitable closure ten years later. It wasn't until 2002 that the

LE QUARTIER DES ANTIQUAIRES

With about 60 secondhand and antique shops, this part of Rue Notre-Dame quickly became known as "the antiques district." Most of the shops sell Victorian or art deco furniture, but you'll also come across specialists in a completely different style, like Lucie Favreau. Retro lovers in search of that rare piece should try their luck on Rue Amherst (Beaudry subway station).

Rue Notre-Dame Ouest, between av Atwater and rue Guy.

canal was reopened for pleasure boating. Along its bank a 9-mile track for cycling and walking has been laid out. A cruise aboard the boat *l'Éclusier* will enable you to learn about its history.

❸ Taverne Magnan★★

2602, rue Saint-Patrick
☎ (514) 935 9647
www.magnanresto.com
Mon.-Fri. 6am-midnight,
Sat. 9am-midnight,
Sun. 9am-11pm.

Taverne Magnan is one of the best known and most popular restaurants in Montreal. In a convivial atmosphere, you can indulge in its specialty: beef! Its roast beef, hung and cooked according to a special recipe, is amazing. Culinary festivals, such as the Lobster Festival (early May to mid-June) and the game festival (September and October), occur throughout the year. Prior reservation is essential.

❹ Ru de Nam★★

2499-2501, rue Notre-Dame Ouest
☎ (514) 989 2002
www.rudenam.com
Mon.-Fri. 11am-2pm,
Tue.-Sun. 6.30-10pm.

Rue de Nam is a Vietnamese restaurant-boutique, chic and refined, right in the heart of the old working-class quarter. You enter through the shop, where decorative objects with an Asian accent are displayed. Then, on your right, is the restaurant where, amid tasteful decor, you can settle down to a delicious Vietnamese meal, piquant and colorful.

❺ Lucie Favreau★

1904, rue Notre-Dame Ouest
☎ (514) 989 5117
Mon.-Fri. 10am-6pm; weekend opening times vary.

Lucie Favreau is a secondhand and antique shop specializing in toys, sports objects and advertisements from the years between 1930 and 1950. The shop overflows with an Aladdin's cave of items, a magnet for the avid collector. Nostalgia reigns supreme!

❻ Spazio★

1700, rue Notre-Dame Ouest
☎ (514) 933 0314
www.spazio.ca
Mon.-Fri. 11am-6pm,
Sat. 11am-5pm.

Installed at the center of an impressive monument of Beaux-Arts inspiration, Spazio offers a unique line in architectural antiques. Both interior and exterior pieces, as well as stylish items of furniture, are on display in an arrangement as subtle as it is unusual.

16

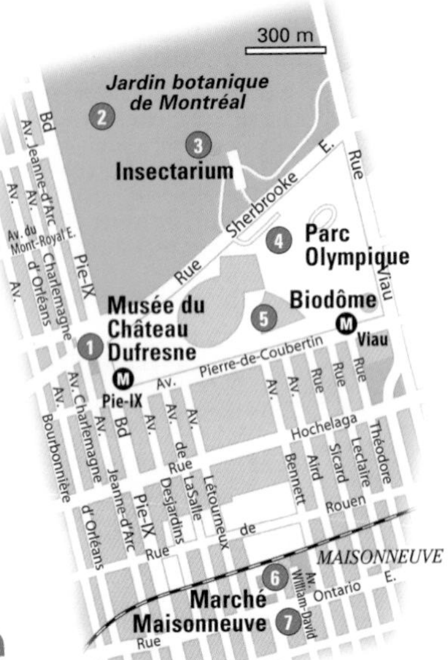

Around Parc Olympique

A little out of the way, but this sector of the Hochelaga-Maisonneuve quarter is an essential for the visitor. You'd be well advised to set aside a whole day, if you want to include several places. It's easy to lose yourself, even along the paths of the Botanical Garden.

❶ Musée du Château Dufresne★

2929, rue Jeanne-d'Arc
☎ (514) 259 9201
www.chateaudufresne.qc.ca
Thu.-Sun. 10am-5pm
Admission charge.

This building in the Beaux-Arts style was erected between 1915 and 1918 by Marius Dufresne and the French architect Jules Renard, and modeled on the Petit Trianon at Versailles. Formerly the Museum of the Decorative Arts (located today within the Musée des Beaux-Arts), Château Dufresne contains a history museum, a visual arts projection room, as well as original furniture surrounded by beautiful murals and ceilings painted by Guido Nincheri.

❷ Jardin botanique★★★

4101, rue Sherbrooke Est
☎ (514) 872 1400
www.ville.montreal.qc.ca/jardin
Jan. to end Oct.: Mon.-Sun. 9am-5pm (until 6pm in summer and 9pm mid-Sep. to end Oct.); Nov. 1-Dec. 24: Tue.–Sun. 9am-5pm
Admission charge, which includes entrance to the Insectarium.
See Don't Miss p. 80.

Covering 185 acres, the Botanical Garden is one of the finest and most important in the world. Nurturing 22,000 plant varieties, it contains ten conservatories and about thirty thematic gardens, including the exotic Chinese and Japanese gardens. Nature lovers will delight in the "Maison de l'Arbre" (House of 'rees), which displays omething of Quebec's rich ndowment of forests.

3 Insectarium★★

4581, rue Sherbrooke Est
☎ (514) 872 1400
Admission charge, which ncludes entrance to the Jardin Botanique.

A real eye-opener, this place will nake you aware of the key role nsects play in the earth's ecological balance. Put aside your phobias, and discover, earn about (and even eat!) these bugs gathered from every corner of the world. An Infozone area allows you to examine their lives in more detail.

4 Parc Olympique★★★

4141, av Pierre-de-Coubertin
☎ (514) 252 4737
www.rio.gouv.qc.ca
Mid-Jun. to end-Aug.: Mon.-Sun. 9am-7pm; Sep. to mid-Jun.: Mon.-Sun. 9am-5pm; guided tours between 11am and 2pm.
Admission charge.

Built to accommodate the summer Olympic Games of 1976, after the designs of French architect Roger Tallibert, the park contains a huge stadium, a sports complex and the famous Tour de Montréal (Montreal Tower). At a height of 570ft and an

angle of 45°, this is the tallest leaning tower in the world (the Tower of Pisa inclines at a mere 5°). By means of a funicular, you can reach the top and enjoy an unforgettable view over the city.

5 Biodôme★★★

4777, av Pierre-de-Coubertin
☎ (514) 868 3000
www.biodome.qc.ca
End Jun. to Sep.: Mon.-Sun. 9am-6pm; Sep. to end Jun.: Tue.-Sun. 9am-5pm
Admission charge.

Opened in 1992, the Biodome is a unique recreation of some of the most valuable ecosystems of the Americas: tropical forest, Laurentian forest, St Lawrence marine life and the Arctic and Antarctic polar worlds. You'll discover a multitude of plants, animals and ponds in climates appropriate to their natural locations. A true museum of the environment!

7 BAIN MORGAN★

The former public baths (1875, av Morgan) of the town of Maisonneuve, this superb structure was built in 1915. Today it encloses a charming swimming pool, much appreciated by local residents.

6 Marché Maisonneuve★

4445, rue Ontario Est
☎ (514) 937 7754
Mon.-Wed. 8am-6pm, Thu. 8am-8pm, Fri. 8am-9pm, Sat.-Sun. 8am-5pm.

This former market building, located on Rue Ontario, was built in 1914, and designed by the architect Marius Dufresne (owner of the Château Dufresne). This market, topped by a delightful dome, was considered one of his most ambitious designs. Nowadays, the public market is located to the right of it, in more modern surroundings. Here you can sample the wares of local farmers.

17

300 m
Lac aux Dauphins
Musée Stewart
4
Fleuve Saint-Laurent
Pont Jacques-Cartier
Île Sainte-Hélène
1
Ch. du Tour-de-l'Isle
Biosphère
M
3
Jean-Drapeau
Passerelle du Cosmos
Pont de la Concorde
Pont des Îles
2
Île Notre-Dame
6 5
Casino de Montréal
Canal de la Rive-Sud
Lac des Régates

Parc Jean-Drapeau

Formed by the two islands of Sainte-Hélène and Notre-Dame, Parc Jean-Drapeau, arena for many special events, is a hub of cultural and sporting activity: swimming, rowing, climbing, canoeing and pedal-boating, concerts, the Latin-American Festival du Merengue, dragon-boat races, ice-skating, a global firework competition and a Fête des Neiges (Snow Festival). Enjoy your vacation!

❶ Île Sainte-Hélène★★★

www.parcjeandrapeau.com

It was to commemorate his wife Hélène that Samuel de Champlain thus christened the island in 1611. In 1820, to protect the country, the British army erected important fortifications here. Then, in 1874, the island was converted to a public park, of which the city of Montreal became the

owner in 1908. The design of the park was entrusted to landscape artist Frederick Todd. Today, in addition to the Biosphere, the Stewart Museum and its woodland, the isle has several points of interest, including the bathing pavilion (a complex of outdoor swimming pools), the Tour De Lévis (a water tower, inspired by the Middle Ages), La Ronde (an amusement park), the fashionable restaurant Hélène de Champlain, not forgetting an impressive sculpture by Alexander Calder.

❷ Île Notre-)ame★★★

vww.parcjeandrapeau.com

n contrast to its cousin, Île Jotre-Dame is completely rtificial. Created to meet the eeds of the Universal xposition (Expo) of 1967, ts construction took 31 nillion metric tons of rock nd earth recycled from the xcavations for the Montreal ubway system. Among its nteresting sights are Montreal Casino, the Gilles Villeneuve 'ormula 1 racing circuit which stages the Canadian Grand Prix each year), the)lympic Pool (built for the Games of 1976), the Floralies Garden and the delightful ittle sandy beach where eople can swim and relax luring the long summer lays.

❸ Biosphère★★

160, chemin Tour-de-l'Isle, le Sainte-Hélène
☎ (514) 283-5000
vww.biosphere.ec.gc.ca
Jun. 1-Sep. 30, Mon.-Sun. 10am-6pm; Oct. 1-May 31, Ved.-Fri. and Mon. 12-5pm, Sat.-Sun. 10am-5pm
Admission charge.

ts impressive dome, designed y architect Richard Buckminster Fuller, is the ormer American pavilion rom Expo 67. Today it houses an environmental observation center and a museum devoted to water, particularly to the St Lawrence River and the Great Lakes. Thematic and interactive exhibition halls make this place both educational and recreational.

❹ Musée Stewart★★

20, chemin Tour-de-l'Isle, île Sainte-Hélène
☎ (514) 861-6701
www.stewart-museum.org
Mid-May to mid-Oct., Mon.-Sun. 10am-6pm; mid-Oct. to mid-May, Wed.-Mon. 10am-5pm
Admission charge.

Housed in the former fort of Île Saint-Hélène, and dedicated to the discovery and exploration of the New World, the Stewart Museum traces four centuries of history by means of old maps and weapons, scientific instruments and navigation aids. Summer and winter, actors in costume bring to life the ambience of a bygone era.

❺ Casino de Montréal★

1, av du Casino, île Notre-Dame
☎ (514) 392 2746
www.casino-de-montreal.com
Open every day 24 hours. 18 or over.

The casino was installed in 1993 in the former Expo 67 pavilions of France and Quebec. The main building, the former French pavilion created by architect Jean Faugeron, has a very interesting interior arrangement, offering a fabulous view of the city. In addition to the multitude of gaming rooms, each evening there are cabaret shows of every variety.

❻ NUANCES★★

Considered one of the best places to eat in town, the restaurant Nuances offers an incomparable view over Montreal and the St Lawrence River. Chef Jean-Pierre Curtat presents a varied and sophisticated cuisine in elegant surroundings. Caviar, lobster and ostrich are some of the items on the menu. You'll need to observe the dress code, though! (Count on spending around $85 for a full meal, including wine.)

Casino de Montréal, 5th floor; ☎ (514) 392 2708; Sun.-Thu. 5.30-11pm, Fri.-Sat. 5.30pm-11pm; 18 or over.

18

A walk outside Montreal

Ideally located, Montreal is only a step away from a variety of places that allow you to escape from the city and renew acquaintance with the charms of nature. Whether you are a sports lover or simply in search of peace and quiet, take a turn in the country and allow yourself a little breathing space!

❶ Parc-nature de l'Île-de-la-Visitation★

2425, bd Gouin Est
☎ (514) 280 6733
www.ville.montreal.qc.ca/parcs-nature
M° Henri Bourassa, then bus no. 69 Est.

Covering an area of 84 acres, this park offers you the possibility of enjoying nature without taking the car! Located on the banks of the Prairies River, its many footpaths permit pleasant walks as well as cross-country skiing in winter (equipment can be rented here). Two historic buildings are located here: La Maison du Pressoir (a former cider press) and La Maison du Meunier (a miller's house), a very romantic terrace café.

❷ La Sucrerie de La Montagne★★★

300, rang Saint-Georges, Rigaud
☎ (450) 451 0831
www.sucreriedelamontagne.com
Telephone or check the Website for directions.

Located 45 minutes from Montreal, La Sucrerie de la Montagne is like a little village in the middle of the forest. An authentic sugar shack, a bakery furnished with a wood stove, little houses where you can spend the night, a dining room with a huge fireplace, and everything built in barn wood. Ideally, you should go there

during "le temps des sucres" (Maple Sugar Time; see p. 18); but traditional and unforgettable tasting festivals take place here all through the year. Definitely an unusual experience!

❸ Lieu historique national du commerce de la fourrure à Lachine★★

1255, bd Saint-Joseph, Lachine
☎ (514) 637 7433
www.parcscanada.gc.ca/fourrure
M° Angrignon, then bus no. 195 to 12th av Lachine
Apr. to mid-Oct., Mon. 1-6pm, Tue.-Sun. 10am-12.30pm and 1-6pm; mid-Oct. to Dec., Wed.-Sun. 9.30am-12.30pm and 1-5pm
Admission charge.

Installed in an 1803 warehouse on the banks of Lac Saint-Louis, this center tells the story of the fur trade, for a long time the principal motor of Canada's economy. Here you will find many exhibits connected with the trade in a hands-on interactive environment.

❹ Écomusée★★

21125, chemin Sainte-Marie, Sainte-Anne-de-Bellevue
☎ (514) 457-9449
www.ecomuseum.ca
Mon.-Sun. 9am-5pm
Telephone or check the Website for directions.
Admission charge.

The Eco-museum is a park of nearly 30 acres, where you can observe animals and plants in their natural habitat. More than 90 species are represented. In contrast to traditional zoos, this park allows you to get close to animals in their own environment.

❺ Parc-nature du Cap Saint-Jacques★★

20 099, bd Gouin Ouest
☎ (514) 280-6871
www.ville.montreal.qc.ca/parcs-nature
M° Côte-Vertu, then buses nos. 64 and 68
Times vary according to season and activities.
Admission charge for beach.

With its 712 acres, this park is one of the most pleasant on the island. In addition to its numerous cycle paths and its forest, the park has a sandy beach beside Lac des Deux Montagnes (Two-Mountain Lake). You will also find a sugar shack and a vast ecological farm, whose fruits and vegetables are on sale in the shop.

❻ Parc national des Îles-de-Boucherville★★

55, île Sainte-Marguerite, Boucherville
☎ (450) 928-5088
www.parcsquebec.com
Access by car.
Bicycles and rackets for hire in the park.
Admission charge.

Composed of a group of small islands in the middle of the river, this park, located only a few miles from downtown Montreal, is a real jewel. Walking and cycling, bird-watching and, especially, canoeing through channels and marshes are the favorite activities. The isle of Grosbois preserves a Native American hut.

ALPINE SKIING

Are you bored with cross-country skiing? Don't worry. You can practice your favorite sport of downhill skiing only 20 minutes away from Montreal. Follow the south bank of the river to Mont Saint-Bruno. Sure, it's not the Alps but to be able to find a ski-slope so close to a major city, you have to admit, is not bad going! (information: ☎ (450) 653-7544). And if this is not challenging enough for you, Mont Tremblant, a 90-minute drive away, might be the answer (information: ☎ (819) 688-2281). Note also that, at Mont Saint-Bruno as well as Saint-Sauveur, you can go skiing at night.

Oratoire Saint-Joseph

Located on the northeast slope of Mont-Royal, St Joseph's Oratory, which welcomes two million visitors each year, is a focus for pilgrimage. You have to climb a hundred or so steps to get to the crypt and almost two hundred more to reach the basilica.

Frère André

The story of Brother André is inseparable from that of the oratory. A porter at Notre Dame College, he devoted his life to people in hardship, invoking the help of St Joseph (patron saint of Canada). Several miracles occurred, and Brother André had a wooden chapel built, in 1904, dedicated to the saint. That building, known as the primitive chapel, was the starting point of the religious complex. In a perpetual quest for more space, the crypt was added in 1917. Its stained-glass windows, created two years later, illustrate scenes from the life of St Joseph.

The basilica

The height of the interior of the building rises to 200ft, and the copper dome is the largest in the world after the one at St Peter's in Rome. This basilica was built between 1924 and 1967 to the plans of Dalbé Viau and Alphonse Venne. The very simple interior decoration encourages the act of prayer. Among the treasures of the basilica are the statues carved out of wood representing the twelve apostles.

Le chemin de croix

A visit to the oratory would be incomplete without passing along the Way of the Cross, one of the loveliest secret gardens in Montreal! Located left of the complex, on the top of the mountain, this place of meditation interpreted, by means of sculpture, the mystery of Christ's Passion. The sculptures were conceived by Louis Parent between 1943 and 1953 and carved by Ercolo Barbieri between 1952 and 1958. They are of natural Indiana stone and marble from Carrara. An interesting fact: The bell tower located to the right of the basilica was to have been installed at the top of the Eiffel Tower!

INFORMATION

3800, chemin Queen-Mary
M° Côte-des-Neiges
☎ (514) 733 8211
www.saint-joseph.org
Mon.-Sun. 6am-10pm.
See p. 65.

Musée d'Art contemporain

Founded in 1964 by the government of Quebec, the Museum of Contemporary Art only became an autonomous institution in 1983, its main mission being to make known, promote and conserve contemporary art in general, and that of Quebec in particular.

Exhibitions

With almost 6,000 works, from 1939 until today, this constitutes the most important collection of contemporary Québécois art. With this rich treasure to draw on, the rooms are regularly rearranged, to present the different works alternately. As well as these, vast spaces are given over to temporary exhibitions. Always impressive, they feature all the recent art movements, such as audio and video installations.

Paul-Émile Borduas

Today recognized for his abstract paintings, Paul-Émile Borduas has had to wait some time before attracting public interest. Born in 1905 in the Montreal area, he became, from the early 1940s, the leader of the "Automatists," a movement that encouraged artistic spontaneity, with the aim of expressing impulses, rather than creating figurative works. Borduas' work marks a turning point in the artistic history of Canada. The museum holds the most important collection of this artist, with 122 works, including 72 paintings.

Sculpture

Sculpture is much in evidence in the museum, which reflects all the major currents of contemporary sculpture, with multiform works utilizing materials as diverse as wood, metal and plastic. The gigantic pine totem pole of Armand Vaillancourt, entitled *Justice for Native Americans* and the *Tour sublunaire* by Ivanhoé Fortier are two good examples. Don't forget to visit the lovely sculpture garden and the attractive museum shop.

INFORMATION

185, rue Sainte-Catherine Ouest
M° Place-des-Arts
☎ (514) 847 6226
www.macm.org
Mon.-Sun. 11am-6pm, (until 9pm Wed.)
Admission charge except Wed. from 6pm.
See p. 52.

Musée des Beaux-Arts

With a collection of more than 30,000 objects, from ancient to modern times, Montreal's Museum of Fine Arts is among the most important in North America. It houses paintings, sculptures, photographs and drawings, as well as examples of decorative art.

Pavillon Jean-Noël Desmarais

Built in 1991 and designed by the architect Moshe Safdie, this building is a remarkable work which has doubled the surface area of the museum. Its many windows admit lots of light to the rooms as well as offering a view of Mont-Royal. On the second floor are the exceptional sculptures of Alexander Calder and Wilhelm Lehmbruck. A network of underground rooms, containing the galleries of ancient culture, joins this pavilion to the second building, the Michal and Renata Hornstein Pavilion.

INFORMATION

1379, et 1380, rue Sherbrooke Ouest
☎ (514) 285 2000
M° Guy-Concordia
www.mbam.qc.ca
Mon.-Sun. 11am-5pm, (until 9pm Wed.), open Mon. in summer.
Admission Charge for temporary exhibitions.
See p. 51.

Old masters

Hung on the second floor of the Desmarais Pavilion, the collection devoted to the old masters is a marvel. It includes works from the Middle Ages up to the end of the 18th century. Don't miss the room devoted to Dutch artists; particularly notable are the paintings of Salome by Godfried Schalcken and *The Duet* by Gerrit van Honthorst. Wonderful early realism!

19th and 20th centuries

These two centuries are represented largely by the Impressionist paintings of Monet, Cézanne and Pissarro, and by more recent works such as Picasso's *Head of a Musketeer* and the sublime *Seated Woman* by Matisse, without forgetting the sculptures of Giacometti and Lipchitz, to mention only two. To complete your visit, linger a moment before the impressive collection of contemporary decorative art (located since 2001 in the pavilion named after the donors, Liliane and David M. Stewart) and in front of the great names of Canadian art, like Jean-Paul Riopelle and Paul-Émile Borduas.

Centre d'Histoire de Montréal

Housed in a former fire station dating from 1903, this little museum is a gold mine for anyone who wishes to dig into the history of Montreal. Two distinct permanent exhibitions present different perspectives on the evolution and daily life of this Québécois metropolis.

Montreal over five epochs

Arranged on the first floor of the building, this exhibition takes you through five stages of history from 1555 to the present day. Each of these periods is depicted in an engaging manner. This journey offers an original vision of Montreal, taking into account the economic, architectural, social and cultural contexts which are the essential foundations for understanding any city.

Interactivity

As well as its educational quality, the great attraction of this museum is undoubtedly its interactivity. Everything has been arranged to reconstitute the atmosphere of the era you are passing through. Audiotapes convey street sounds, music and historical narratives, and the models, objects, drawings and images are displayed on wall panels or rotating triangular columns. Finally, each room provides a quiz with questions that will deepen your knowledge at the same time as keeping you amused.

Montreal of a hundred faces

Located on the second floor, this exhibition presents another view of the city: that of its inhabitants. Many Montrealers, of various ages and backgrounds, speak about their town, of the areas that give life to it, of the different cultures that live side by side in it, and of their working experiences. These witnesses present their accounts from video screens installed within various living spaces, from the office to the kitchen. An original and absorbing piece of theater direction!

INFORMATION

335, place d'Youville
☎ (514) 872 3207
M° Place-d'Armes
www.ville.montreal.qc.ca/chm
May-Aug., Mon.-Sun. 10am-5pm; Sep.-Apr., Wed.-Sun. 10am-5pm
Admission charge.
See p. 42.

Jardin botanique

The Botanical Garden is a dream come true for lovers of nature, and it is best to set aside a whole day to enjoy it to the full. Created in 1931 by Frère Marie-Victorin, it remains one of the city's most popular locations.

Exhibition greenhouses

Located near the entrance, these are among the garden's star attractions. In the course of a colorful visit, you pass through a diverse universe, comprising a tropical forest, a collection of orchids and arums (there are more than 1,500 species of these), a "celestial garden" (which includes an important collection of penjings, or Chinese dwarf trees), a begonia greenhouse, a Mexican hacienda and tropical plants that are used for food or medication. The large exhibition greenhouse has a regular change of program. The Pumpkin Ball organized at Halloween is spectacular.

Chinese Garden

Opened in 1991, it is still the largest Chinese garden outside China. Inspired by the gardens of the Ming dynasty, it was created entirely in China, before being shipped across piece by piece and reassembled here. Seven pavilions surround the "lake of dreams" amid lush vegetation: magnolias, bamboo, lotus and peonies. From September until Halloween, the garden is open at night for the "Magic of Lanterns," more than 750 of them.

Japanese Garden

Spread across 6 acres, this thematic garden enables you to learn something in a natural way of the Japanese philosophy of landscape gardening. Stone and water, which dominate the space, encourage a feeling of peace and serenity. A huge pavilion, inspired by traditional family

houses, stages various exhibitions as well as an introduction (in summer) to the Japanese tea ceremony. Not to be missed is a magnificent collection of bonsai (the oldest is 370 years old) and an amazing stone garden.

INFORMATION

4101, rue Sherbrooke Est
M° Pie-IX
☎ (514) 872 1400
www.ville.montreal.qc.ca/jardin
Jan. to end-Oct., Mon.-Sun. 9am-5pm (until 6pm in summer and 9pm from mid-Sep. to end Oct.); Nov. 1-Dec. 24 Mon.-Sun. 9am-5pm.
Admission charge.
See p. 70.

Parc du Mont-Royal

More than just a park, Mont-Royal is a symbol, one of the city's landmarks. A magical place which, thanks to its height, offers unforgettable panoramas, it is a haven of peace much cherished by Montrealers.

Frederick Law Olmsted

Born in the state of Connecticut in 1822, Frederick Law Olmsted, though self-taught, is the most famous landscape architect in America. Fascinated by nature, he traveled the world and, at the age of 35, was appointed as superintendent of New York's Central Park, before becoming its architect. Then he embarked on numerous large-scale projects, including the design of Mont-Royal. Wishing to preserve the natural charm of the place, he created a long and winding road (which today bears his name) that allows you to reach the highest point in the park while taking in its beauty on the way.

Treasure mountain

After all, there are so many beautiful things to see! With more than 110,000 trees of 60 different species, Parc du Mont-Royal is like an arboretum in the heart of town. White pines, silver maples, American linden trees and red oaks border the many footpaths. You will also find 150 species of birds, a quantity of rare plants such as wood garlic and small mammals like raccoon and skunk.

Smith House

This is the information center for the park. Built in 1858, the Smith House, a true architectural relic, contains a permanent exhibition called "Monte Real, Monreale, Mont Royal, Montréal." The whole story of the development and conservation of this legendary location is recounted here.
☎ (514) 843 8240
Mon.-Fri. 9am-5pm
(until 7pm weekends and public holidays in summer).

INFORMATION

M° Mont-Royal then bus no. 11 West
☎ (514) 843 8240
www.lemontroyal.qc.ca
See p. 64.

Plateau Mont-Royal

Called the Plateau because it is elevated in comparison to downtown Montreal, this is one of the most fashionable and desirable areas of the city. Its narrow tree-lined streets and village ambience invite you to stroll at leisure.

A brief history

At the end of the 19th century, the villages of Côteau-Saint-Louis, Saint-Jean-Baptiste and Saint-Louis-du-Mile-End formed this area that is today so highly prized. The villages had been set up to receive the Quebecers coming from the countryside to work in the nearby quarries and tanneries. Houses adorned with balconies, terraces and little gardens enabled them to find a way of life similar to their previous one. The alleyways running along the back of their houses also provided an opportunity for sociability.

Charm and character

Plateau Mont-Royal took its present shape at the turn of the 20th century. The houses, of typical Montreal architecture, mold themselves into the landscape: duplex dwellings of two or three stories, divided into several apartments. Built in rows, the houses have only two sides exposed to the cold, so are well insulated in winter. A picturesque feature of this district is the outside stairways. The municipality requires builders to leave a distance of about 3 meters between the house and the edge of the street. So, in order to give more room to the inside of the house, the stairways are installed on the sidewalk. Various shapes and colors give each stairway a character of its own.

Strolling

The architecture and the atmosphere here are equally agreeable. Each street has its charm. As you stroll along Rue Fabre (see p. 59), as far as Avenue Laurier, you will imbibe the village atmosphere, an impression continued in the delightful Parc La Fontaine with its countryside air.

INFORMATION

From rue Sherbrooke in the south to av. Laurier in the north, and from Mont-Royal in the west until av. Papineau in the east.
M° Sherbrooke, Mont-Royal and Laurier.
See p. 58.

Pointe-à-Callière

It's because the nobleman Louis Hector de Callière, Montreal's third governor, built his home here in 1688 that the museum is so called. In addition to its archeological wealth, the museum mounts shows that focus attention on the city's unique heritage.

Architecture

The museum is composed of three structures. The main building, L'Éperon (The Spur), was erected in 1992 on the spot where the town was founded 350 years before. Its tower and its triangular shape recall the prow and crow's nest of a sailing ship, thereby proclaiming its proximity to the Old Port. Even though it's an ultramodern building, its simplicity accords perfectly with the Old Town. Its construction attracted several architectural prizes for its designer, Dan S. Hanganu.

Built in1836, then enlarged in 1881, the former Custom House has not changed. Today it houses exhibitions and the museum shop (see p. 123). The Youville pumping station, an important part of the industrial heritage, is on its far side (at no. 173).

Archeological crypt

Located underneath Place Royale, it houses the remains of fortifications and buildings constructed in the 17th, 18th and 19th centuries. The museum was created as a result of important archeological discoveries made in the 1980s. More than a millennium of human activity is preserved in this basement, including the remains of Montreal's first Catholic cemetery, dating from 1643. As well as ruins, you will see models presenting the development of Place Royale, as well as historic artifacts and a multimedia presentation on Place du Marché.

Rare spectacle

Virtual technology is encroaching everywhere! Submit to the magic with "If Montreal had told me," an astounding spectacle that retraces the city's history in a theatrical setting integrated with the newest techniques. Comfortably seated in a large hall above the ruins, let yourself go on this amazing journey through time (lasting 18 minutes).

INFORMATION

350, place Royale
M° Place-d'Armes
☎ (514) 872 9150
www.pacmusee.qc.ca
Mon.-Fri. 10am-5pm,
Sat.-Sun. 11am-5pm,
(until 6pm Jul. and Aug.)
Admission charge.
See p. 42.

Le Vieux-Port

Because of its geographical location, Montreal has always been an important port. Since 1976, however, its industrial activity has moved farther to the east. After several redevelopment projects, the Old Port today is devoted to recreational and leisure activities.

History

Although the first harbor works began in 1763, it was only in 1830, shortly after the opening of the Lachine Canal and just as the formidable industrial development of the city was starting to accelerate, that the port began to assume its full splendor. By the end of the 19th century, with its docks, sheds, quays and grain silos, Montreal had become the center of maritime transportation in Canada. In 1922, the Tour de l'Horloge (Clock Tower) was erected in homage to the sailors who had lost their lives in the First World War. Nowadays it is the emblem of the Old Port.

Sport and leisure activities

Far removed from its industrial past, the Old Port's main activity today is recreational. Most of the warehouses have been converted into leisure areas, the river is now the embarkation point for pleasure boats and the waterfront is endowed with a lovely garden. In summer, bicycles and rollerblades occupy the space, while in winter the crowds make their way down to Bonsecours Basin, metamorphosed into an enormous skating rink (equipment can be rented there).

Centre des sciences

Opened in 2000, the Science Center is not a museum so much as an interactive complex of science and amusement. Aimed at the whole family, it seeks to familiarize the public at large with modern technology, through the medium of thematic displays which teach and entertain at the same time. Here you can see the IMAX movie theater, whose screen is the equivalent of a seven-story building.
☎ (514) 496 4724

INFORMATION

M° Place-d'Armes or Champ-de-Mars
www.vieuxportdemontreal.com
See p. 42.

Basilique Notre-Dame

uilt between 1672 nd 1683, the first lotre Dame church, ecause of lack of pace, had soon to be eplaced. With its mposing presence, he new basilica, onstructed between 824 and 1829, enabled he Catholic religion to ssert its importance mong the myriad 'rotestant churches merging around it.

'he interior

the outward appearance f the basilica already affirms s architectural grandeur, its nterior décor, the work of ne architect Victor Bourgeau, magnificent. The reponderance of carved wood including the marvelous ulpit made of black walnut) nd of color define its tmosphere. In addition, the urquoise vaults constellated vith golden stars, reminiscent f those in Paris's Sainte-hapelle, are dazzling! At the ar end is a magnificent asavant organ dating from 891 and comprising 7,000 ipes, the tallest of which is 0 meters high.

The choir

'his is a masterpiece. In ontrast to the modesty that ome religious buildings go in for, the choir of the basilica flaunts itself and radiates its glory from all angles. Painted, then plated with gold leaf, the high altar is made of black walnut and its statues of pine. They recall the Eucharist, one of the seven sacraments. The six multicolored sculptures, installed each side of the altar, are of plaster. They represent the four evangelists enclosed between St Peter and St Paul.

Chapelle de Sacré-Coeur

Constructed between 1888 and 1891, for the celebration of marriages, the Chapel of the Sacred Heart was partly destroyed by fire in 1978. Its reconstruction has allowed the ancient and the modern to be merged with great ingenuity. Your gaze will be caught by the magnificent bronze high altar representing the various stages of life. This work by the sculptor Charles Daudelin weighs at least 22 tons! Also note the original way that shafts of natural light are introduced above the vault.

INFORMATION

110, rue Notre-Dame Ouest
M° Place-d'Armes
☎ (514) 842 2925
www.basiliquenddm.org
Mon.-Fri. 8am-4.30pm,
Sat. 8am-4.15pm,
Sun. 12.30pm-4.15pm
Admission charge
See p. 44.

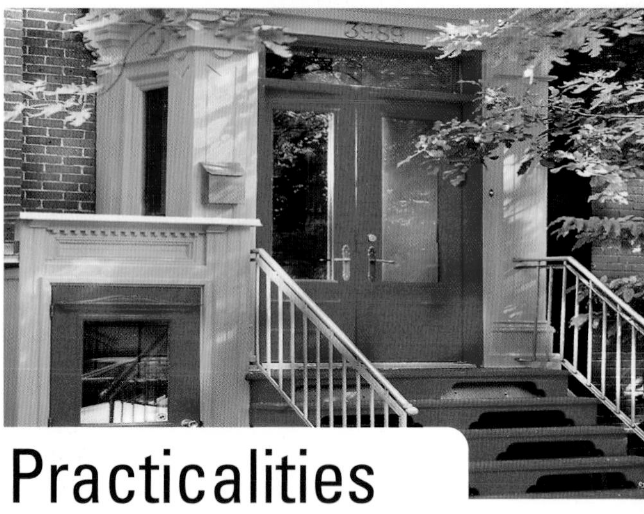

Practicalities

Hotels

Montreal has a choice of hotels wide enough for all tastes and all budgets. In effect, 25,000 rooms are available, either in the downtown area, where you will find modern, luxurious accommodation as well as the big international chains (Hilton, Marriott, Novotel), in Vieux-Montréal, the area of private hotels of charm and prestige, and, finally, if you prefer the personalized welcome of a bed and breakfast place, you will find them grouped, for the most part, around Rue Saint-Denis, in the Latin Quarter, or in the Plateau Mont-Royal district. To grade these establishments, this guide follows the usual classification system:

★★★★★: exceptional comfort, superbly appointed, first-class service, nothing is too much trouble
★★★★: superior comfort, finely appointed, full range of services
★★★: very comfortable, very well appointed, many services
★★: comfortable, adequately furnished, some services

Reservations

Since Montreal plays host to numerous conferences and festivals, you'd be well advised to make your reservations in advance, especially in the months of June and July in the weeks of the Canadian Grand Prix and the International Jazz Festival. If you are a smoker, you must mention it when reserving your room. In general, the hotels have many no-smoking zones: the whole building, in some cases. To make a reservation, it's often best to contact the hotel directly, as hotels sometimes have special rates or attractive packages, particularly in the low season from November through April. Or you could go to the tourist office, which often has special deals at interesting prices throughout the year.

Tourisme Montréal
☎ (514) 873 2015
Ⓕ (514) 864 3838
www.tourisme-montreal.org

BRING YOUR OWN

Although some restaurants are not licensed to sell alcohol, they are authorized to let their customers bring their own. Generally speaking, a notice "Apportez votre vin" (bring your own wine) is displayed by the entrance. This practice is fairly common in Montreal, and allows you to drink and be merry at a cheaper rate than otherwise.

₹oom rates

enerally speaking, and earing in mind the shifting xchange rates between the anadian dollar and the US ollar or pound sterling, :aying in Montreal is not all ıat expensive. For about 130, you can find a omfortable and tastefully ırnished room. Remember, ıough, that the advertised rices do not generally ıclude taxes. You have to dd to them the federal tax TPS) of 7 percent and uebec sales tax (TVQ) of 7.5 ercent. Federal tax can be eclaimed by non-residents see p. 101). Lastly, there is n accommodation tax of $2 . night. In most stablishments, breakfast is ıcluded in the price, but ome places only provide it vith rooms of superior uality, so be sure to inquire n advance. And, in order to void a disagreeable surprise vhen you go to check out, be ure to ask in advance about our telephone bill.

Restaurants

ccurately reflecting its emographic make-up, Montreal has more than 80 ypes of cuisine from across he world. Low-budget estaurants stand alongside amous establishments, such ıs Toqué! or Anise, for gourmets only. Quebecers line early, from 5.30pm onwards (like the rest of North America), and during winter some restaurants may close early, or even take an extra day's holiday! So emember to check in advance. For your nformation, breakfast is called *déjeuner* ("lunch" in France), lunch is called *dîner* ("dinner") and the evening meal is called *souper* ("supper"). But don't worry: Montrealers are well accustomed to these language differences! In the evening, most establishments offer a fixed-price menu, commonly called the *table d'hôte*. In general, it's advisable to make a reservation for the evening meal, especially if you're traveling in high season (May through September).

Prices

For the sake of consistency, we have used the same method of grading for restaurants as we used for hotels. The number of stars relates to the amount you would expect to pay, corresponding to the average price for a dinner for one person, excluding tax and drink. The classification, then, is as follows:

★★★★: more than $60
★★★: from $30 to $60
★★: from $15 to $30
★: less than $15

Remember that prices printed on the menu do not include tax. You have to add the TPS and TVQ (see left), which will increase your bill by about 15 percent. And, since service is not included, you will have to leave extra for the tip. The standard amount for this is 15 percent of the bill, not counting the tax. If you're paying by credit card, you simply add it directly to the bill, beside the space for *pourboire* (tip). If you're paying by cash, leave the tip on the table.

FINDING YOUR WAY

You will find details of the nearest metro station (M°) after the address in the Rooms and Food section.

Hotels

1 - *Hôtel Le St-James*
2 - *Les Passants du Sans Soucy*
3 - *Auberge Le Jardin d'Antoine*
4 - *Auberge Pierre du Calv*

Vieux-Montréal

Auberge-Restaurant Pierre du Calvet★★★★

405, rue Bonsecours
M° Champ-de-Mars
☎ (514) 282 1725
🅕 (514) 282 0456
www.pierreducalvet.ca
Double room $250 to $275, breakfast included.

The walls covered with carpets, the wood paneling, the antiques and the marble bathrooms have earned this hotel, dating from 1725 and comprising nine rooms, a prodigious reputation. Breakfast is served in a Victorian conservatory, and the establishment also possesses a top-of-the-range restaurant considered one of the best in town.

Auberge du Vieux-Port★★★★

97, rue de la Commune Est
M° Champ-de-Mars
☎ (514) 876 0081
🅕 (514) 876 8923
www.aubergeduvieuxport.com
Double room $175 to $245, breakfast included.

Perfectly located by the St Lawrence River, this five-story hotel has 27 rooms (non-smoking) with solid wood floors walls of original brick and cast iron bedsteads. A superb roo terrace and the restauran Les Remparts, which serve excellent French cusine, hav recently been added. Eacl evening an aperitif of wine anc cheese is served.

Hôtel Nelligan★★★★

106, rue Saint-Paul Ouest
M° Place-d'Armes
☎ (514) 788 2040
🅕 (514) 788 2041
www.hotelnelligan.com
Double room $190 to $295, breakfast included.

The Nelligan Hotel (namec in honor of the poet) is a little esthetic jewel. A central atrium allows the double salon/library warmed in winter by a crackling fire in the hearth, to be illuminated by natural light. Its 63 rooms, including 28 suites, have tasteful contemporary decor (fireplace and jacuzzi in every suite). The recently opened roof-terrace bar as well as the fitness room and the excellent Verses restaurant (see p. 92) add to the charm of this hotel.

Les Passants du Sans Soucy★★★

171, rue Saint-Paul Ouest
M° Place-d'Armes
☎ (514) 842 2634
🅕 (514) 842 2912
www.lesanssoucy.com
Double room $115 to $175, breakfast included.

Located in a former warehouse dating from 1723, this delightful three-story hotel, completely non-smoking, is composed of nine rooms with stone walls, exposed beams, cast-iron bedsteads, a whirlpool bath and antique furniture. The height of romanticism! The breakfast of omelets and croissants is deservedly famous.

Auberge Bonsecours★★★

353, rue Saint-Paul Est
M° Champs-de-Mars
☎ (514) 396 2662
🅕 (514) 396 5138
www.aubergebonsecours.com
Double room $160 to $175, breakfast included.

An excellent refuge if you're looking for calm and serenity above all else. Built in the heart of former stables, the seven rooms of this hotel are grouped round an inner courtyard. Their decoration blends the charm of ancient stonework with the exoticism of furniture with more than a suggestion of India. A large outside terrace enables guests to take advantage of fine weather.

Rue Saint-Jacques square Victoria

Hôtel Le St-James★★★★★

355, rue Saint-Jacques
☎ (514) 841 3111
🅕 (514) 841 1232
www.hotellestjames.com
M° Square-Victoria
Double room $400 to $475, breakfast not included.

It's not by chance that this hotel is installed in the heart of a famous building in the financial

district. A real shop window of all that's luxurious, the St James comprises 23 rooms and 38 suites all furnished with antiques and works of art from around the world. The lobby and the grand salon (what a pleasure to take tea there!; see p. 98) are in the same mold. But most impressive of all is the spa, whose combination of stone walls and chandeliers plunges you into a unique ambience.

Hôtel Saint-Paul★★★★

355, rue McGill
M° Square-Victoria
☎ (514) 380 2222
🅕 (514) 380 2200
www.hotelstpaul.com
Double room $215 to $290, breakfast included.

The façade of the former Canadian Express building is in stark contrast to the interior of avant-garde luxury. The St Paul Hotel is a triumph of modern design, the work of Spanish-born Ana Borrallo. The translucent alabaster fireplace near the entrance will give you a foretaste. The 96 rooms of simple but refined decor all possess a marble washbasin, CD player, broadband Internet, fax and mini-bar. In all, there are 24 rooms, as well as a bar, restaurant and fitness center.

Hôtel Gault★★★★

449, rue Saint-Hélène
M° Square-Victoria
☎ (514) 904 1616
🅕 (514) 904 1717
www.hotelgault.com
Double room $229 to $549, breakfast included.

Opened in 2002, this establishment of 30 rooms, determinedly modern, has been designed with enormous care, blending various colors and shapes to give each room its own identity. Some of them have a terrace, and they are all provided with CD and DVD players, flat-screen TVs, broadband Internet, a mini-bar and a heated bathroom floor.

Centre-ville

Hôtel Maritime Plaza★★★★

1155, rue Guy
M° Guy-Concordia or Lucien-L'Allier
☎ (514) 932 1411
🅕 (514) 932 0446
www.hotelmaritime.com
Double room $144 to $184, breakfast not included.

This enormous hotel of 210 rooms provides every modern comfort. Certain floors are non-smoking, so be sure to specify the type of room you want. An indoor swimming pool, an

exercise room, a gift shop, as well as a terrace are at the disposal of guests.

L'Hôtel de la Montagne★★★★

1430, rue de la Montagne
M° Peel
☎ (514) 288 5656
Ⓕ (514) 288 4027
www.hoteldelamontagne.com
Double room about $200, breakfast included.

L'Hôtel de la Montagne is one of the little treasures of the downtown area. Its panoramic terrace, located on the 20th floor, offers a swimming pool, bar and restaurant once the fine weather arrives. The spacious rooms open onto balconies. All the bathrooms contain a separate bath and shower.

Le Nouvel Hôtel★★★

1740, bd René-Lévesque Ouest
M° Guy-Concordia
☎ (514) 931 8841
Ⓕ (514) 931 5581
www.lenouvelhotel.com
Double room $129 to $170, breakfast included depending on price of room.

Located close by the Canadian Center for Architecture (see p. 15) and Rue Crescent, this establishment of 126 rooms and 40 studios is very good value for money. The guests' comfort and well-being are given priority, with an outdoor swimming pool, a fitness room, a hairdressing salon and a bar. The rooms are welcoming, even though the bathrooms might be thought small.

Hôtel Y de Montréal★★

1355, bd René-Lévesque Ouest
M° Lucien-L'Allier or Guy-Concordia
☎ (514) 866 9942
www.ydesfemmesmtl.org
Double room (with bathroom) $75 to $85.

Completely renovated in 2003, and run by the Women's Y Foundation of Montreal, this hotel offers those on low budgets the chance of accommodation right in the center of town. Its 66 rooms are plain but comfortable, most of them with private bathrooms. The hotel also has an indoor pool (for women only) and cooking facilities.

Latin Quarter

Angelica Blue Bed & Breakfast★★★★

1213, rue Sainte-Hélène
M° Berri-UQAM or Champ-de-Mars
☎ (514) 844 5048
Ⓕ (514) 448 2114
www.angelicablue.com
Double room $85 to $145, breakfast included.

A furnished apartment and five variously themed rooms are available. High ceilings, walls of brick and real wood floors contribute to the charm of the place. An equipped kitchen is at your disposal. But be warned: The building is entirely non-smoking and does not allow you to wear shoes (slippers are supplied).

Couette et Café Cherrier★★★★

522, rue Cherrier
M° Sherbrooke
☎ (514) 982 6848
www3.sympatico.ca/couette
Double room $60 to $105, breakfast included.

Not far from Parc La Fontaine, this bed-and-breakfast has four comfortable rooms (with television and air conditioning), within a building one hundred years old. Two of them have private bathrooms. Lounge and fireplace are located on the second story, while a terrace ideal for sunbathing has been installed on the top floor.

Hôtel des Gouverneurs Place Dupuis★★★★

1415, rue Saint-Hubert
M° Berri-UQAM
☎ (514) 842 4881
Ⓕ (514) 842 8899
www.gouverneur.com
Double room $139 to $184, breakfast included depending on the price of the room.

Hôtel des Gouverneurs is good value for four-star accommodation. Furnished with direct access to Berri-UQAM subway station (very convenient on wintry days!), it offers spacious, comfortable rooms (ask for a view over the downtown area). Staff are very

1 - *À la Maison de Pierre & Dominique*
2 - *L'Hôtel de la Montagne*
3 - *Hôtel Gault*
4 - *Hôtel des Gouverneurs Place Dupuis*

welcoming, and you can take advantage of the indoor swimming pool, sauna, fitness center, bar and restaurant.

Auberge Le Jardin d'Antoine★★★

2024, rue Saint-Denis
M° Berri-UQAM
☎ (514) 843 4506
(514) 281 1491
www.hotel-jardin-antoine.qc.ca
Double room $88 to $167, breakfast included.

Close to the bars, restaurants and shops of Rue Saint-Denis, this delightful hotel of 25 rooms (only two of which overlook the street) is a friendly and relaxing place. Each room is decorated in a different style, and some of them have a bathroom with jacuzzi. A small flower-filled courtyard at the back offers an ideal retreat.

À la Maison de Pierre et Dominique★★

271, square Saint-Louis
M° Sherbrooke
☎ (514) 286 0307
www.bbcanada.com/928.html
Double room $75 to $100, breakfast included.

St Louis Square is considered one of the finest in Montreal. Staying here makes you feel that your trip is already a success! Pierre and Dominique have transformed their house into a bed-and-breakfast that focuses on the pleasure of their guests. They offer three rooms for non-smokers, as well as a marvelous breakfast, and are happy to share the secrets of their city with you.

Plateau Mont-Royal

Auberge de La Fontaine★★★

1301, rue Rachel
M° Mont-Royal
☎ (514) 597 0166
(514) 597 0496
www.aubergedelafontaine.com
Double room $120 to $224, breakfast included.

At the foot of the famous Parc La Fontaine, this charming little hotel comprises 21 cheerful and modern rooms. Each incorporates a private bathroom, a workspace and cable television.

Restaurants

1 - Boris Bistro
2 - Chez L'Épicier
3 - Thaï Express
4 - Piccolo Diavolo

Vieux-Montréal

Chez L'Épicier★★★

311, rue Saint-Paul Est
M° Champ-de-Mars
☎ (514) 878 2232
Mon.-Fri. 11.30am-2pm and 5.30-10pm, Sat.-Sun. 5.30-10pm.

This establishment is a unique space, incorporating the old stonework of Vieux-Montréal in an ultramodern setting. Both a delicatessen and a restaurant, its chef Laurent Godbout offers a sophisticated cuisine replete with the flavors of Quebec. The desserts – *club sandwich au chocolat*, for example – are original and delicious.

Verses Restaurant★★★

100, rue Saint-Paul Ouest
M° Place-d'Armes
☎ (514) 788 4000
Mon.-Fri. 11am-2pm, Sun.-Thu. 5.30-10.30pm, Fri.-Sat. 5.30-11pm.

Housed within the magnificent building of the Nelligan Hotel, Verses Restaurant presents contemporary French cuisine occasionally accented with nuances of extra sweetness. The welcome is warm, and the setting, both chic and up-to-date has quickly made this place one of the most fashionable and popular eating places in town. If you have the time, it's worth prolonging your visit by taking a nightcap on the roof terrace.

Boris Bistro★★

465, rue McGill
M° Square-Victoria
☎ (514) 848 9575
Mon.-Fri. 11am-11.30pm, Sat.-Sun. noon-11.30pm. Hours variable in winter.

On fine days, everyone heads for

oris Bistro, to enjoy its onderful outdoor terrace ıeltered from the street by an ıormous stone façade. It's the leal place to lunch or dine tête--tête. The cuisine is simple but aried, ranging from duck andwich to grilled swordfish. he inside of the restaurant is qually convivial.

Centre-ville

.e Commensal★★

204, av McGill College
1° McGill
☎ (514) 871 1480
1on.-Sun. 11.30am-10pm.

egetarians, rest assured: A hain of restaurants is edicated to you! With the food resented in the form of a uffet, you can snack here, at ny time of the day, on quiches, alads, mixed fried vegetables nd bean curd soup. The esserts are widely renowned, nd even meat-eaters will epart happy!

Latin Quarter/ Village

Mikado★★

731, rue Saint-Denis
M° Berri-UQAM
☎ (514) 844 5705
un.-Mon. 5.30-10pm,
ue.-Thu. 5.30-10.30pm,
ri.-Sat. 5.30-11pm.

n essential address for lovers of ushi. Justly considered by Montrealers to be one of the best in town, this Japanese restaurant, whose decor could not be more ordinary, offers a range of sushi and maki. Specialty of the house: a blend of raw fish and tempura seasoned with a sweet aromatic sauce. Perfect!

Piccolo Diavolo★★

1336, rue Sainte-Catherine Est
M° Beaudry
☎ (514) 526 1336
Mon.-Fri. 11.30am-2pm,
Mon.-Sun. 5-11pm.

With an interior that blends fantasy and color with sophistication, the "Little Devil" offers you high-quality Italian cooking. There are the traditional dishes of pasta, pizzas and grills, but also an excellent *table d'hôte* is offered each evening, when the chef doesn't think twice about adding certain Québécois ingredients to his recipes. The *osso buco* of venison and spaghetti *aux têtes de violons* form part of this agreeable culinary adventure.

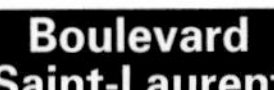

Boulevard Saint-Laurent

Thai Express★

3710, bd Saint-Laurent
M° Sherbrooke
☎ (514) 287 9957
Mon.-Fri. 11am-10pm,
Sat.-Sun. 11am-11pm.

It's not often that a budget restaurant owes its reputation to its quality decoration and the esthetic of its dishes. But that is the case here. This Thai restaurant welcomes you in an atmosphere worthy of Maxim's and offers generous portions of tasty authentic dishes. Those of you with delicate palates, beware! The food is on the hot side.

Buonanotte★★

3518, bd Saint-Laurent
M° Sherbrooke or Saint-Laurent; ☎ (514) 848 0644
Mon.-Wed. 11.30am-midnight, Tue.-Sat. 11.30am-1am,
Sun. 5pm-midnight.

Buonanotte is one of the hottest addresses on Boulevard Saint-Laurent. In an atmosphere noisy

QUEBEC FLAVORS

Lovers of good authentic restaurants will enjoy Au Pied de Cochon (Pig's Trotter; p. 58) for its succulent grills, and Le Cabaret du Roy (p. 41) for its exploration of an earlier epoch. Those in search of a quick, inexpensive (but good-quality) snack should try the famous La Binerie Mont-Royal for its bacon and beans (367, av du Mont-Royal Est) or the fast-food chain La Belle Province for its impressive *poutines* (481, rue Sainte-Catherine Ouest).

rather than chic, you can eat some amazingly tasty Italian cooking. The entrées come in big portions, and some splendid cheese dishes can be ordered from the menu. From 8.30pm onwards, the decibels rapidly mount. A DJ or background music set the rhythm for the evening.

BU★★

5245, bd Saint-Laurent
M° Laurier or bus no. 55
☎ (514) 276 0249
Tue.-Fri. 12-2am, Mon. and Sat. 5pm-2am
Non-smoking.

Located on the fringe of the Outremont district, this wine bar and trattoria offers a deliciously tasty selection of dainty aperitifs and cold entrées to be eaten with a glass of wine. The menu lists thirty or so wines by the glass (about $18 for a trio), and many more by the bottle. Each evening, a plate of pastries and a *plat de jour* (daily special) are added to the menu. An elegant spot, calm and convivial, it's an ideal place for winding down at the end of the day.

Plateau Mont-Royal

L'Express★★/★★★

3927, rue Saint-Denis
M° Sherbrooke
☎ (514) 845 5333
Mon.-Fri. 8am-2am, Sat. 10am-2am, Sun. 10am-1am.

The unusual look of this French brasserie (black and white mosaic floor, and decor based on a dining car) doubtless contributes to its reputation. If you develop a yearning for steak and French fries or roast chicken, or even for the lively, smoke-filled atmosphere of a Paris bistro, you'll be glad you found L'Express, a restaurant much appreciated by the Montreal crowd. But if you don't want to experience Paris-on-the-St Lawrence, you'd better go elsewhere!

Un Monde Sauté★★

1481, av Laurier Est
M° Laurier
☎ (514) 590 0777
Wed.-Fri. noon-2pm, Tue.-Sat. 5.30-10pm.

The chef's idea is simple: to be influenced by the cuisines of the entire world, as long as every dish is *sauté* (lightly fried). Thus the flavors of Asia, Italy, France and South America feature together here, to the gratification of your taste buds. The lunchtime portions are very generous, and the evening menu offers great value for money. This is an ideal restaurant that is every food-lover's dream!

Chez Doval★★

150, rue Marie-Anne Est
M° Mont-Royal
☎ (514) 843 3390
Mon.-Sun. noon-midnight.

This is the perfect place to pass a warm and lively evening in the company of friends. Chez Doval is a Portuguese restaurant specializing in charcoal grills. Meat and fish (the braised chicken is the star of the menu!) sizzle away behind the counter diffusing a mouth-watering aroma around the room. And when the holiday mood is at its height, the chef brings out his guitar. A Montreal moment!

Outremont

Anise★★★★

104, rue Laurier Ouest
M° Laurier; ☎ (514) 276 6999
Tue.-Sat. 6-10.30pm.

1 - *Verses Restaurant*
2 - *Anise*
3 - *Verses Restaurant*
4 - *Un Monde Sauté*

Anise is one of Montreal's top restaurants. In an extremely subdued interior, the chef Racha Bassoul creates dishes that are virtual works of art. Two menus composed of *petites attentions* (small portions of exquisitely prepared food) are on offer. They comprise between six and nine dishes ($65 to $90) hinting of subtle Mediterranean flavors. Some of the dishes can be ordered separately.

Les Chèvres★★★★

1201, av Van Horne
M° Outremont
☎ (514) 270 1119
Mon.-Sun. 5.30-10.30pm.

Vegetables take pride of place in this impressive restaurant that uses only organic produce and meat from carefully raised animals. Fillet of duck with macerated raisins, piquant mushroom stew, Portobello mushroom pâté with tarragon: each item is full of flavor, naturally prepared with assiduous attention to detail.

Au Cyclo★★

5136, av du Parc
M° Laurier, bus no. 80 or 129
☎ (514) 272 1477
Tue.-Fri. 11.30am-2.30pm, Tue.-Thu. and Sun. 5.30-10pm, Fri.-Sat. 5.30-11pm.

Located on the first floor, this unpretentious Vietnamese restaurant provides delicious authentic cuisine at a very reasonable price. You will receive a warm welcome, and savor the traditional soups and the famous Bo-Bun, composed of rice vermicelli, bean sprouts, thin strips of beef marinated in a blend of lemon grass, coriander and *nuoc mam* (fish sauce). Pure delight!

AND ALSO...

Conveniently located near some of the places you will visit: gastronomic menus at Toqués! (p. 45) and Nuances (p. 73); the height of cool at the Newtown (p. 51); a culinary voyage at Milos (p. 63), Ru de Nam (p. 69), Ben's Delicatessen (p. 49), and Schwartz's (p. 55); a breathtaking view from the lofty Altitude 737 (p. 47); and a genuine workers' tavern at Magnan's, with its enormous steaks (p. 69).

Light meals

2

3

4

1 - Café Santropol
2 - Céramic Café Studio
3 - Olive+Gourmando
4 - L'Anecdote

Vieux-Montréal

Titanic

445, rue Saint-Pierre
M° Square-Victoria
☎ (514) 849 0894
Mon.-Fri. 7.30am-4pm.

Installed discreetly in a basement, Titanic offers original sandwiches, quiches, salads, a selection of hors d'oeuvres, as well as daily specials (the *chilli con carne* is a favorite). If possible, avoid going there at mid-day (between noon and 1.30pm): the wait can be very long!

Olive+Gourmando

351, rue Saint-Paul Ouest
M° Square-Victoria
☎ (514) 350 1083
Tue.-Sat. 8am-6pm.

This café-bakery is a fixture in Vieux-Montréal. Some tables, in the "bread and cakes" corner, are set apart from the meal counter. The menu includes sandwiches of unexpected types (smoked trout and dried tomatoes, goat's-milk cheese with caramelized onions), soups, salads and various other dishes. Leave space for the desserts: they're well worth the effort.

Céramic Café Studio

95, rue de la Commune Est
M° Champ-de-Mars
☎ (514) 868 1611
Mon.-Sun. 11am-9pm.

A café serving light meals linked to a ceramic painting studio: This is an original idea which allows you to create your pottery (cups, plates, vases) while you eat. The atmosphere is very convivial, the decor has overtones of Provence, the panini bread is excellent, and the St Lawrence River is floating past! Relax, you're on holiday!

Downtown

Eggspectation

1313, bd de Maisonneuve Ouest
M° Peel
☎ (514) 842 3447
Mon.-Sun. 6am-5pm.

With its typically American feel, Eggspectation is one of the most popular places for weekend brunch. There are egg dishes galore, and a grand choice of waffles and pancakes. Nothing too sophisticated, but good, traditional North American fare. Try the Waffle Benedict or the classic Uneggspected.

Mangia

1101, bd de Maisonneuve Ouest
M° Peel
☎ (514) 848 7001
Mon.-Fri. 7.30am-7pm, Sat. 9am-5pm.

Mangia is more of a grocery store than a restaurant (a few tables on the terrace, a small number inside). It offers some quality dishes sold by weight: pasta salads, meat strips, grilled vegetables, plates of fruit and various sandwiches. A good place for a quick bite, or to pick up food for a picnic in the park.

Latin Quarter/ Plateau Mont-Royal

Café Cherrier

3635, rue Saint-Denis
M° Sherbrooke
☎ (514) 843 4308
Mon.-Fri. 7.30am-1am, Sat.-Sun. 8.30am-11.30pm.

Well-established, the Café Cherrier with its big sun-drenched terrace attracts hordes of Montrealers. It offers light bar meals served in a friendly atmosphere. An excellent place for brunch, its eggs Benedict with smoked salmon and its homemade compotes are exceptional.

Byblos

1499, av Laurier Est
M° Laurier
☎ (514) 523 9396
Tue.-Sun. 9am-11pm.

Discover the joys of traditional Middle Eastern cuisine. In a simple Persian-style interior, you can sample *boranis* (a mixture of yoghurt and vegetables), *koukous* (baked omelets) and other specialties including Iranian cakes and pastries, accompanied by mint tea. A delicious experience at a ridiculously low price.

Café Santropol

3990, rue Saint-Urbain
M° Sherbrooke, bus no. 29 or 55
☎ (514) 842 3110
Mon.-Sun. 11.30am-midnight.

You come here for the surroundings as much as for the food. With a little garden and a lake, Café Santropol is a real haven of peace. The interior decor, with its Mexican flavor, contributes to the effect. They serve sandwiches, some rather original: for example, ham with mint, apple and cucumber, or coriander with mayonnaise, grape, apple and grated carrot.

L'Anecdote

801, rue Rachel Est
M° Mont-Royal
☎ (514) 526 7967
Mon.-Fri. 7.30am-10pm, Sat.-Sun. 9am-10pm.

An important place on the Plateau! In an atmosphere half American-diner, half café-retro, you will find some incredible hamburgers. Lamb with blue cheese and mushrooms, venison with goat's cheese, smoked bison and mustard, or veal with cheese, curry and mushrooms are among the best. You should also try the *crêpes* (thin pancakes) with their equally far-out flavors.

Soupesoup

80, rue Duluth Est
M° Sherbrooke, bus no. 29 or 55
☎ (514) 380 0880
Mon.-Fri. 10am-9pm, Sat. 10am-5pm.

The menu varies daily according to the manager's choice and what's available at the market. It all results in a delicious selection of hot or cold soups. Some of the classic soups are here, of course, as well as surprising combinations like cold beetroot soup with a hint of orange. And the homemade cakes are just as lovingly made.

AND ALSO...

For more ideas, see details of Café des Éclusiers (p. 43) and Café Italia (p. 61).

Coffee, tea and cakes

1 - Le Bilboquet
2 - Hôtel Le St-James
3 - Les Délices de L'Érable
4 - Les Délices de L'Érable

Nocochi

2156, rue Mackay
M° Guy-Concordia
☎ (514) 989 7514
Mon.-Fri. 9am-9pm, Sat.-Sun. 9am-8pm.

Discreetly tucked beneath the Musée des Beaux-Arts, this café-pâtisserie provides a perfect escape from the crowds. Decorated all in white, it encourages calm and relaxation. Nocochi skillfully fashions miniature cookies, whose appearance is as good as their taste. Chocolate, almond and strawberry, vanilla, hazelnut or apricot, these exquisite delicacies go perfectly with your coffee. You can eat them here or take them with you.

Le Bilboquet

1311, av Bernard Ouest
M° Outremont
☎ (514) 276 0414
Every day 7am-midnight in summer; 7am-10pm rest of the year.

This is without doubt the most popular ice-cream parlor in Montreal. Its tiny shop leaves little space for eating on the spot, but what does that matter when the parks are so handy (see p. 62)? Among the specialties of th[e] house are the *chocouett[e]* (chocolate and peanut butter), *king kong* (chocolate an[d] banana) and *cacaophoni[e]* (cashew nuts and whit[e] chocolate) flavors, and from March through mid-May, during Maple Sugar Time, maple-syrup ice cream is served. If you want to keep the calories at bay, try mango and coconut, blueberry or lime sorbets.

Hôtel Le St-James

355, rue Saint-Jacques
M° Square-Victoria
☎ (514) 841 3111
Mon.-Sun. 2-5pm.

The gracious St James Hotel (see p. 89) serves high tea daily in the purest English tradition. It's true

AND ALSO...

For details of more treats, see Maison Cakao (p. 59) and La Croissanterie Figaro (p. 63).

hat the decor is ultrachic and he service a bit stiff but, let's face , it's nice to be waited on! he tea is served with homemade cones (with cream and jam), ea cakes and raspberries. For hose who really want to make meal of it, there is an expanded econd version, enriched with an ssortment of mini-sandwiches, oie gras and caviar (about $45). he Ritz-Carlton Hotel, which as an indoor garden, offers the ame teatime service (1228, rue herbrooke Ouest).

Les Délices de l'Érable

34, rue Saint-Paul Est
M° Champ-de-Mars
☎ (514) 765 3456
Mon.-Sun. 10am-10pm.

deally located in the heart of Vieux-Montréal, this outlet offers only products based on maple syrup, and it's a sugar fiend's paradise! First of all, there are the nimitable cakes – like sugar tart, blueberry muffin, banana and maple syrup mousse – as well as excellent chocolate cookies. Afterwards, try the ice creams with unusual flavors of strawberry, mint and basil, blueberry, lychee, maple or meringue. In short, an agreeable pause for a snack, accompanied – why not? – by a cup of maple tea.

Salon de Thé 0-Cha-I

4669, rue Saint-Denis
M° Mont-Royal
☎ (514) 982 9229
Tue.-Wed. 11.30am-11pm, Thu.-Sat. 11.30am-midnight, open Mon. in summer.

Far from the formality of the St James, this Asiatic teahouse provides a Zen-like aura of tranquility. The menu offers teas from around the world, including a delicate white peony tea, authentic Indian tea and Moroccan green tea. To accompany this soothing beverage, there are some exotic pastries that can take your breath away: green-tea tiramisu, Earl Grey crème brûlée or azuki-bean rolls. An Oriental pleasure dome.

Moozoo

133, rue de la Commune Est
M° Champ-de-Mars
☎ (514) 878 1222
Every day 11am-9pm (sometimes later) Apr.-Oct.; only weekends rest of the year.

If the summer humidity overwhelms you, and you think that a little cool pick-me-up might be in order, head for Moozoo. Blends of fruit, frozen yoghurt (or, rather, yoghurt ice cream) and every kind of juice are there to slake your thirst. As imaginative as they are practical, little bottles of natural and refreshing drinks are on sale, based on fruits whose names and colors may surprise you.

Kilo

1495, rue Sainte-Catherine Est
M° Beaudry or Papineau
☎ (514) 596 3933
Sun.-Fri. 11am-11.30pm, Sat. 11am-0.30am.

The slices of cake are as tall as they are broad, and bear evocative names such as Tourbillon Framboise (raspberry whirl), Tarzan, Skor, Choco-Blues and even Bart Simpson. The mousses, cheesecakes and other sweets have helped give this Quebec enterprise a great reputation for pastry-making. The café, with its whimsical window display, offers a perfect break to the dedicated cake enthusiast.

A CAFÉ SOCIETY

You will find one at the corner of every street, offering a wide variety of coffees (espresso, latte, iced), as well as cakes and other drinks to consume on the spot or take away. Among the big Canadian chains, Second Cup and Café Dépôt are very popular and observe high standards. If you prefer places with a bit more individuality, Café CC Crème is one to remember (1219, rue Sainte-Catherine Est).

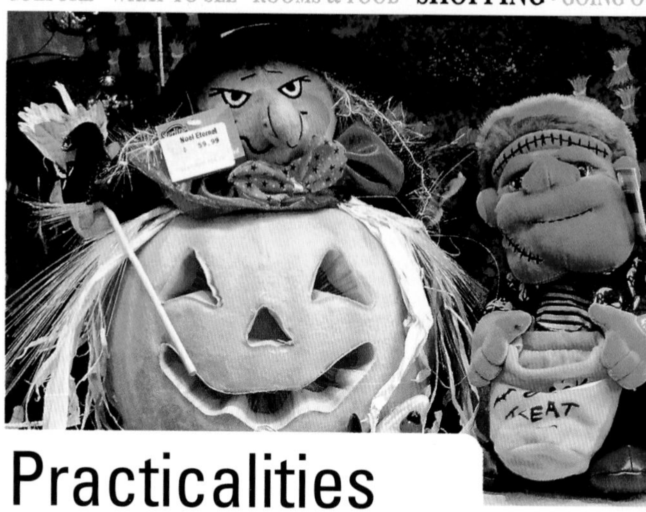

Practicalities

Where to go shopping

Rue Sainte-Catherine – between Rue Guy and Rue Berri – is the main shopping area of Montreal. Essentially, what you'll find there are fashion outlets, souvenir and novelty boutiques, and big stores such as La Baie and Ogilvy, as well as numerous entrances to the various subterranean malls.
The other main shopping artery is Rue Saint-Denis (between Boulevard Maisonneuve and Avenue du Mont-Royal). Many young designers have set up shop there, as well as life-style boutiques and stores devoted to interiors and sports. Stores focusing on design and contemporary furniture are clustered on the Boulevard Saint-Laurent.

For antiques, it's best to walk along Rue Notre-Dame Ouest – between Guy and Atwater – or Rue Amherst for everything retro – between Sainte-Catherine and Sherbrooke. Finally, mothers will beat a fond path to Westmount, with its many stores on Rue Sherbrooke devoted to children – between Grey and Lansowne. Remember, though, that every district nurtures its own little shopping treasures. In the course of your ramblings, you may unearth some pleasant surprises.

Opening hours

In general, the shops open at 10am (sometimes a little earlier on Saturdays) and at noon on Sundays.
They close at 6pm Monday through Wednesday (5pm at weekends), and stay open Thursday and Friday evenings until 8 or 9pm.
In winter, some shops set their own opening times. Check beforehand.

How to pay

Stores and businesses take most bank and credit cards. Traveler's checks are generally accepted in hotels and some large shops, but it's advisable to change them at a bank as soon as you arrive. If you want to withdraw cash, ATM machines can be found at most banks. It sometimes

FINDING YOUR WAY

You will find details of the nearest metro station (M°) after store addresses in this Shopping section.

happens that they won't accept all cards, but that's exceptional.

If you lose your bank card

You should telephone (free) to the following numbers:
Visa
☎ 1 (800) 847 2911
American Express
☎ 1 (800) 869 3016
Master Card
☎ 1 (800) MC-ASSIST (62 277478)

Tax refund

The prices stated on price tags are exclusive of tax. When you come to pay, the federal tax (TPS) of 7 percent, as well as the Quebec sales tax (up to 7.5 percent), will be added. As a non-resident of Canada, you can reclaim the federal tax for every purchase equal to, or exceeding, $50 (before tax). To do this, it is imperative that you keep your receipts and fill in a form obtainable from the customs, at tourist offices, or downloaded from the Internet (see web address below):

Agence des douanes et du revenu du Canada
www.cra-arc.gc.ca/visiteurs/
☎ (800) 668 4748
(free call)

Global Refund Canada
Centre Eaton de Montréal
☎ (514) 847-0982

For all additional information, contact the tourist office in Montreal at:
☎ (514) 873 2015.

Sales

Unlike in Europe, there is no law regulating the period of sales, and the shops set the dates themselves at the end of each season. In general, winter sales begin on Christmas Eve and continue to the end of January. Boxing Day (December 26) sees some significant price reductions,

and a sea of humanity pours into the downtown stores as soon as they open. Apart from these classic sales, the city (or its trade associations) organizes numerous "sidewalk sales" from early May through late September. In most cases, the streets are closed to traffic to leave more space for these temporary markets. The atmosphere is very friendly, and you can pick up some real bargains. Among the most important are those on Boulevard Saint-Laurent – between Rue Sherbrooke and Avenue du Mont-Royal – the second half of June and the end of August; and that on Rue Sainte-Catherine – from Rue Atwater to Rue Saint-Urbain – around the middle of July. For a precise calendar of these events, contact the Montreal tourist office (see p. 35).

Pharmacies and convenience stores

Montreal pharmacies – like those in North America generally – are real Aladdin's caves. You'll find your pharmacy requirements there; they are often open late at night. But don't forget the convenience stores (*dépanneurs*) found all over town, for any other immediate purachses (see p. 36).

A BRIEF REMINDER

Don't forget that there are certain disparities between European norms and North American ones. In general, for every small electronic item you purchase (MP3 player, digital camera, camcorder, and so on), a simple adapter will enable you to use your appliance in Europe. On the other hand, some equipment will require a transformer. Be sure to make the necessary inquiries when you make your purchase. Also, remember that Canadian DVDs are made for zone 1, and will only work if your DVD player is multi-zone.

Women's fashion

Window-shoppers will find themselves at home in Montreal. All kinds of ready-to-wear stores spring up everywhere, and on Rue Sainte-Catherine alone you will have so much to occupy you that a whole day will scarcely suffice. Among this plethora of stores, there are some Canadian brands and Québécois designers worth noting, and here is a sample.

Tristan & America

1001, rue Sainte-Catherine Ouest
M° Peel
☎ (514) 982 9480
www.tristan-america.com
Mon.-Wed. 10am-6pm, Thu.-Fri. 10am-9pm, Sat. 9am-5pm, Sun. noon-5pm.

Founded in Montreal in the 1970s by Denise Deslauriers and Gilles Fortin, this chain of stores – today spread across the whole of North America – sells clothing for men and women: Tristan for her, America for him. Models of elegance and femininity, classic but always original styles, comfortable and varied materials, colors skillfully matched: in short, these fashions unite sophistication and simplicity, for everyday wear.

Scandale

3639, bd Saint-Laurent
M° Sherbrooke or bus no. 55
☎ (514) 842 4707
Mon.-Wed. 11am-6pm, Thu.-Fri. 11am-9pm, Sat. 11am-5pm, Sun. noon-5pm.

Its colorful window display is bound to catch your attention. So much the better! Scandale features the magical creations of George Lévesque. This self-taught couturier, responsive to the diverse currents of modern fashion, invents inspired retro dresses, combining supple and luxurious material in a way that emphasizes a woman's sensuality in a tasteful way. Absloutely must be seen.

Dubuc Mode de Vie

4451, rue Saint-Denis
M° Mont-Royal
☎ (514) 282 1465
www.dubucstyle.com
Mon.-Wed. 10.30am-6pm, Thu.-Fri. 10.30am-9pm, Sat. 10.30am-5pm, Sun. 1-5pm.

It was only in autumn 2000 that Philippe Dubuc, a former men's fashion designer (see p. 105), applied himself to the feminine sphere.
His creations, top of the range in their simplicity, focus on detail and choice of materials, combined in unheard-of ways – cotton with metal, for example. Subdued colors, cloth that is draped and weightless: the "Dubuc woman" wants to be elegant, while remaining discreet.

Jacob

1220, rue Sainte-Catherine Ouest
M° Peel
☎ (514) 861 9346
Mon.-Fri. 10am-9pm, Sat. 10am-5pm, Sun. noon-5pm.

You'll be happy to discover this line of Canadian garments, comfortable and finely tailored, at exceptional prices.
The T-shirts (from $20), sweaters and cardigans are available in a variety of colors, and will find a place in anybody's wardrobe. Don't miss the lingerie section in the basement: it contains some interesting surprises.

Muse

4467, rue Saint-Denis
M° Mont-Royal
☎ (514) 848 9493
www.muse-cchenail.com
Mon.-Wed. 10.30am-6pm, Thu.-Fri. 10.30am-8pm, Sat. 11am-5pm, Sun. noon-5pm.

Before entering the fashion world, Christian Chenail first trained as an architect, and this has greatly influenced the way he conceives his designs. He accords great

importance to the structure of a garment, excluding all superfluous decoration.
In short, these are classic styles with original cuts, for everyday wear as well as for special occasions.

Kaliyana

4107, rue Saint-Denis
M° Mont-Royal
☎ (514) 844 0633
www.kaliyana.com
Mon.-Wed. 10am-6pm, Thu.-Fri. 10am-9pm, Sat. 10am-5pm, Sun. 11.30am-5pm.

Kaliyana is a very unusual shop. Its creator, Jana Kalous, presents basic clothes, of a full cut, with a sobriety that resembles a sort of Japanese minimalism. You can wear them one at a time or all together. The idea is that with six different pieces you can put together twenty different permutations! An innovative idea that will make getting dressed virtually a work of art (about $150 each item).

MARIE SAINT PIERRE

Marie Saint Pierre's shop is a fount of new ideas. She is without doubt the most modern of the Quebec designers, daring to give to her creations an air of sport and culture combined that perfectly represents today's woman. Lively colors, shimmering materials from silk organza to microfiber, via seersucker and tulle, everything is planned so that the wearer will shine. It's also worth casting your eye on the original collection in crease-resistant taffeta, sold in plastic tubes: an excellent idea for the journey home.

2081, rue de la Montagne
M° Peel
☎ (514) 281 5547
www.mariesaintpierre.com
Mon.-Wed. 9.30am-6pm, Thu.-Fri. 9.30am-8pm, Sat. 9.30am-5pm, Sun. noon-5pm.

Men's fashion

It's hard to define the men's fashion you see on the streets of Montreal. Definitely less showy than the Italians, without declining into outright indifference, the men here prefer an informal style that's typically North American. But that doesn't at all frustrate the talents of brilliant young creators like Philippe Dubuc or the Mandels, who know how to offer their clients great elegance that is 100 percent Québécois.

L'Uomo Montreal

1452, rue Peel
M° Peel
☎ (514) 844 1008
www.luomo-montreal.com
Mon.-Wed. 9am-6pm, Thu.-Fri. 9am-8pm, Sat. 9am-5pm.

Supporters of the suit that's both classic and fashionable, this is your shop! Here there is no extravagance, just sobriety with a dash of refinement. The big European couturiers are represented, including Ermenegildo Zegna and Cerruti. And to take elegance to its utmost possible height, you must add the little accessory that will make all the difference: a cap from James Lock, some John Lobb moccasins or some cufflinks from Links.

Kamkyl

439, rue Saint-Pierre
M° Square-Victoria
☎ (514) 281 8221
www.kamkyl.com
Mon.-Wed. 11am-6pm, Thu.-Fri. 11am-8pm, Sat. 10am-6pm, Sun. 11am-5pm.

The stylish Kamkyl fashions aim to hit the note of laid-back elegance: long cashmere coats, leather jackets, velvet jackets. The suits made of high-quality material (linen, silk, wool, etc.) are altogether exceptional. Yvonne and Douglas Mandel, designers of this Montreal brand, have

succeeded in giving to their creations an aspect both smart and accessible (we won't talk about the price!).

ANOTHER WORLD

An attractive space dedicated to smart and funky sportswear. Out with the suit and tie, and on with the T-shirt, the jeans and the pants of many pockets. Italian fashion dominates the shop, with brands like Energie, FDN (Fabio di Nicola), whose shoulder bags are much sought-after, and even Diesel. And, as well as its famous off-the-peg collections, Diesel offers its line in shoes and underwear. It's enough to make the women go green with envy!

1302, rue Sainte-Catherine Est
M° Beaudry
☎ (514) 521 0101
Mon.-Wed. 10am-7pm, Thu.-Fri. 10am-9pm, Sat. 10am-6pm, Sun. 11am-6pm.

Dubuc Mode de Vie

4451, rue Saint-Denis
M° Mont-Royal
☎ (514) 282 1465
www.dubucstyle.com
Mon.-Wed. 10.30am-6pm, Thu.-Fri. 10.30am-9pm, Sat. 10.30am-5pm, Sun. 1-5pm.

Philippe Dubuc is without doubt the best known male designer in Canada. In 1993, he created his first line, which introduced a new tone to urban fashion. As with his women's fashions (see p. 102), he favored black and white colors over livelier hues. His styles often hug the body: tight trousers and jackets with prominent shoulders. The quiet sobriety of his collections is highly prized in Montreal.

La Casa del Habano

1434, rue Sherbrooke Ouest
M° Guy-Concordia
☎ (514) 849 0037
www.lacasadelhabano.ca
Mon.-Wed. 10am-8pm, Thu.-Fri. 10am-9pm, Sat. 10am-6pm, Sun. noon-5pm.

If you're one of those who have to stifle a groan when shopping is mentioned, here perhaps is an address that might reconcile you to this onerous activity. Located close to the Musée des Beaux-Arts, La Casa del Habano offers you a choice of genuine Cuban cigars in a smart and convivial atmosphere. Ensconced in a comfortable leather armchair, you can savor your favorite Havana cigar and sip a cup of Cuban coffee. You can also take advantage of the wide choice of accessories and magazines relevant to the art of cigar-smoking.

For children

What mother does not yearn to buy a unique outfit for her adorable cherub? What parent has not hunted high and low for a little plaything to make their infant smile? You will come across all sorts of kids' stores on your way, but the highest concentration of shops for children is on Rue Sherbrooke, in the residential district of Westmount.

Oink Oink

1343, av Greene
M° Atwater
☎ (514) 939 2634
www.oinkoink.com
Mon.-Fri. 9.30am-6pm, Sat. 9.30am-5pm, Sun. 11am-4pm.

Two shops devoted to children, with parlor games, toys, clothes, books and gadgets. So, if you have a gift to buy, you'll be able to find a rare pearl in this Aladdin's cave. For the very young, see the crocheted footwear by Padraig Cottage (about $30), while the seamless sleeping suit, of incredibly soft spandex, will melt the heart of many a mother.

La Grande Ourse

129, rue Duluth Est
M° Sherbrooke or Mont-Royal; ☎ (514) 847 1207
Wed. noon-6pm, Thu.-Fri. noon-9pm, Sat.-Sun. noon-5pm.

For supporters of wooden toys and environmental awareness, La Grande Ourse (Great She-Bear) will be like an oasis in the middle of a desert. Marguerite Doray, the proprietor, will gently and passionately explain to you the educational value of each object, such as the little rings specially invented to help babies develop their teeth. Another idea for a gift:

some ravishing little woolen figures, and some larger dolls made of natural materials.

Alpaqa

533, rue Duluth Est
M° Sherbrooke or Mont-Royal
☎ (514) 527 9687
www.alpaqa.com
Mon.-Wed. and Sat. 10am-6pm, Thu.-Fri. 10am-9pm, Sun. 10am-5.30pm.

This shop, for sure, is not just for children. But who would not weaken before this collection of clothes and accessories made of 100 percent alpaca? This wool, taken from the hair of the Andean mammal, is one of the softest and warmest on the planet. So, to approach winter without trepidation, why not wrap baby in an authentic little Peruvian pullover and bonnet? You know you can't resist.

La Petite Ferme du Mouton Noir

1298, rue Beaubien Est
M° Beaubien
☎ (514) 271 9760
Mon.-Wed. 10am-6pm, Thu.-Fri. 10am-8pm, Sat. 10am-5pm.

A bit out of the way, this shop, the Little Farm of the Black Sheep, nevertheless merits a visit. Its young Québécoise designer offers a line of undemonstrative and well-conceived clothing for the very young and for adolescents (from birth to 16 years). The textures are comfortable (the hooded sweatshirts with raglan sleeves are superb!), and the patterns are bright and cheerful. See, for instance, the lovely little flowery dresses. Count on spending about $24 for a baby's T-shirt.

Lmnop

4919, rue Sherbrooke Ouest
M° Vendôme
☎ (514) 486 4572
Mon.-Fri. 10am-6pm, Sat. 9.30am-5pm, Sun. noon-5pm.

Many families inhabit the residential district of Westmount, which no doubt explains the abundance of boutiques for children. This one, with its alphabetical name, contains many articles ideal for the open air. Nozone overalls built-in with sun protection, an incredible collection of rubber boots, swimming costumes, sunglasses: everything your children will need for their next vacation is here.

PEEK A BOO

This colorful shop is above all else a secondhand clothes store - for children from 0 to 8 years – much appreciated by Montreal mothers. It's their only chance to sell the clothes of the baby who's grown out of them, and to search for some more at a bargain price, perhaps out of the ravishing designs of the Quebec brand Deux Par Deux (Two by Two). Some new items are also sold, such as Robeez shoes and Do-Gree hats. And the children enjoy the atmosphere here, where they are the sole focus of attention!

807, rue Rachel Est
M° Mont-Royal
☎ (514) 890 1222
www.friperiepeekaboo.ca
Mon.-Fri. 10am-6pm, Sat. 10am-5pm, Sun. noon-5pm.

Youth styles
and sportswear

Montreal is everyone's idea of a shopper's paradise, especially if you are young. Whether you are a victim of the latest fashion trends or are simply looking for new jeans and trainers, you are sure not to leave empty-handed. Rue Sainte-Catherine – as always – can fulfill any young person's retail dream, however far out. And if the sky is gray and full of rain, you can always seek shelter in the underground malls.

Parasuco

1414, rue Crescent
M° Peel
☎ (514) 284 2288
www.parasuco.com
Mon.-Wed. and Sat. 9.30am-6pm, Thu.-Fri. 9am-9pm, Sun. noon-6pm.

Established in the Montreal region in 1975 by Salvatore Parasuco, this enterprise specializes in jeans of its now world-famous brand. Housed in the magnificent building of a former bank, the store concentrates on selling sex appeal: low-slung pants, tight leather jackets, sequined blouses, backless dresses. Parasuco sets its sights on making you – and its clothes – the center of attraction, and you have to admit it works!

Jacob Connexion

360, rue Sainte-Catherine Est
M° Berri-UQAM
☎ (514) 842 9357
Mon.-Fri. 10am-9pm, Sat. 10am-5pm, Sun. noon-5pm

A younger offshoot of Jacob (see p. 103), Jacob Connexion focuses more on sportswear, with particular emphasis on

:ans and unisex styles. You'll nd the shortest of short shorts r summer, a wide range of ooded sweatshirts (about 30), sleeveless T-shirts in variety of colors, and the atest line in canvas belts. n short, a cool and expensive collection of ady-to-wear fashion, ncluding some basic ssentials to enliven any ardrobe!

Jrban Outfitters

246, rue Sainte-Catherine uest
M° Peel
☎ (514) 874 0063
www.urbanoutfitters.com
Mon.-Fri. 10am-9pm, Sat. 0am-5pm, Sun. noon-5pm.

egendary among 15 to 25 ear olds, this concept store hain now owns 65 shops cross North America. In the avernous space of its two oors, you can find all you ver dreamed of: clothes, hoes, jewelry, books, gadgets, abrics, ornaments and ccessories, hats and unglasses. The trend is hippie hic, even peace and love, but resistible even so.

American Apparel

001, rue Saint-Denis
M° Sherbrooke
☎ (514) 843 8887
www.americanapparel.net
Mon.-Wed. 10am-6pm, Thu.-Fri. 10am-9pm, Sat. 0am-5pm, Sun. noon-5pm.

merican Apparel is the brand f American T-shirts that verybody wears and that a arge number of budding esigners use as a base on which to stamp their own articular style. Created by Dov Charney, a native of Montreal, he business is now established n Los Angeles, where it makes ll its products.

There's nothing fancy in its styles, all having only one or two colors, but the cotton used is of an impeccable softness. True classics (about $22 for a man's T-shirt).

Mavi

1241, rue Sainte-Catherine Ouest
M° Peel
☎ (514) 843 6284
www.mavi.com
Mon.-Fri. 10am-9pm, Sat. 9am-5pm, Sun. 11am-5pm.

You will no doubt be surprised to learn that this brand of jeans, becoming increasingly desriable, is of Turkish origin. Throughout the world, young people and fashion freaks are snapping up Mavi's designs, in which the cloth – somewhat finer than that of its competitors – and the cut – daringly low-cut and sexy – have become the height of fashion. There are also some delectable flounced skirts.

Fidel

3525, bd Saint-Laurent
M° Sherbrooke
☎ (514) 286 5151
www.fidelclothing.com
Mon.-Wed. and Sat. 11am-6pm, Thu.-Fri. 11am-9pm, Sun. noon-6pm.

This young brand of Montreal street clothing is easily recognized, with its brightly colored T-shirts with eye-catching logos on the chest. Here's a psychedelic lion (in the Fidelknights line), for instance, and there goes the silhouette of a boxer. Watch out, too, for the pretty dresses, the jeans, sweaters and accessories. Impossible not to feel cheerful.

AND IN PREVIEW…

Many North American brands and Québécois designers don't yet have their own premises. Their products are sold from various stores, and it would be a pity to miss them. Here are some useful addresses:

Indigo (Havanaias sandals and Free People clothing)
4920, rue Sherbrooke Ouest, M° Vendôme or bus no. 24

James (Mme Woo lingerie and C&C California T-shirts)
4910, rue Sherbrooke Ouest, M° Vendôme or bus no. 24

Nahika (Québécois designers such as Glas Gow)
4435, rue Saint-Denis, M° Mont-Royal

Haus (Jesse May brand and Spiewak garments)
372, rue Sherbrooke Est, M° Sherbrooke

Accessories

It's true that Montreal won't topple the Italians from their position as kings of footwear (and of leather generally), nor will they overtake the French in the way of saucy silk underwear. But not to worry: there's always jewelry. In this domain you'll find a multitude of craftspeople whose creativity will amaze you. Moreover, museum shops have many little treasures on sale. And if you prefer real diamonds, Henry Birks (intersection of Carré Phillips and Rue Sainte-Catherine) should make you sparkle.

Rudsak

1400, rue Sainte-Catherine Ouest
M° Guy-Concordia
☎ (514) 399 9925
www.rudsak.com
Mon.-Wed. 10am-6pm, Thu.-Fri. 10am-9pm, Sat. 10am-5pm, Sun. noon-5pm.

Launched in 1994 in Montreal by the designer Evik Asatoorian, Rudsak makes clothes and accessories in leather of very high quality. Long coats for women, made of fine and supple skin, cling snugly to the body. The colors of the purses are anything but timid: bright red, yellow and sky blue make them easy to find in the dark. And gizmo lovers will be in their element: Take the rainbow-hued wallets, for instance.

Aqua Skye

2035, rue Crescent
M° Peel
☎ (514) 985 9950
www.aquaskye.com
Mon.-Wed. 11am-6pm, Thu.-Fri. 11am-9pm, Sat. 11am-5pm, Sun. noon-5pm.

You could easily pass by this tiny boutique without seeing which would be a pity. For inside you will find the jewelry creations of many Québecois designers: leather collars, necklaces adorned with feathers, earrings of fantastic size, rings made of

recycled material, and for those whose ears have not bee pierced, Sylvie Germain has created a marvelous line of ear clips inspired by ancient jewelry.

a Senza

133, rue Sainte-Catherine
uest
I° Peel
☎ (514) 281 0101
'ww.lasenza.com
lon.-Fri. 10am-9pm,
at. 10am-7pm,
un. 10am-5pm.

npossible to avoid this anadian underwear empire - it owns no less than 200 :ores across Canada as well s many others worldwide. ure, it's more agreeable to uy where no-one else does, ut when you can get a avishing nightdress nsemble for $12, who's omplaining? Value for noney is exceptional, and he choice is wide. Look ut for casual housecoat utfits for slouching round at home.

Aldo

Centre Eaton
705, rue Sainte-Catherine
Ouest
M° Peel
☎ (514) 842 3144
☎ (514) 286 1412
www.aldoshoes.com
Mon.-Fri. 10am-9pm,
Sat. 10am-5pm,
Sun. noon-5pm.

Another Canadian enterprise with a firm reputation, Aldo Bensadoun creates shoes and accessories for the whole family. The men's styles are

simple but flattering (about $90), and the low-fronted ladies' shoes are offered in a variety of colors. Jewelry, fashionable but inexpensive, has recently been added to the range.

Chapofolie

3944, rue Saint-Denis
M° Sherbrooke
☎ (514) 982 0036
Mon.-Thu. 11am-6pm,
Fri. 11am-9pm,
Sat. 11am-5pm,
Sun. 1-5pm.

Seek out this address to find the headgear of your dreams! The designers are Québécois, for sure, but they offer a considerable choice, from mesh or nylon caps to bowler hats, not to mention the plain or flowery cloches and the evening numebrs with lace and feathers. Moreover, the service is charming. The hardest thing will be to make your choice.

Shan Femme

2150, rue Crescent
M° Peel
☎ (514) 287 7426
www.shan.ca
Mon.-Wed. 10am-6pm,
Thu.-Fri. 10am-9pm,
Sat. 9.30am-5pm,
Sun. noon-5pm.

Chantal Lévesque welcomes you to her charming boutique entirely devoted to women! Here is a space dedicated to the joys of swimming and sunbathing, with a selection of top-of-the-range bathing suits. The perfect fit and attention to detail typical of the designs – feathers, veils, jewels, belts – make these items truly unique. Count on spending about $170 for a set.

HARRICANA PAR MARIOUCHE

The creations of Mariouche Gagné are made from recycled materials. Her main focus is fur. By using of old, discarded material (including fur), gathered here and there, she creates ravishing and entirely original accessories, such as mesh bonnets with fox-fur pompoms, or deerskin boots layered with mink. Not content with recycling fur, she also uses old scarves brilliantly to make elegant tank tops.

3000, rue Saint-Antoine Ouest , M° Lionel-Groulx
☎ (514) 287 6517
www.harricana.qc.ca
Mon.-Fri. 10am-6pm, Sat. 10am-5pm,
Sun. noon-5pm.

Health and beauty

In Montreal, and Quebec generally, natural products are much in favor. Aromatherapy, essential oils, flowers, plants, fruits: Montrealers are great believers in using the gifts of nature. Let yourself be tempted by this abundance of authenticity, and discover the way to a healthier life.

Fruits et Passion

4159A, rue Saint-Denis
M° Mont-Royal
☎ (514) 282 9406
www.fruits-passion.com
Mon.-Fri. 10am-9pm,
Sat.-Sun. 10am-5pm.

Fruits et Passion is a Canadian brand that offers ecologically sound products with a fruity aroma. Its esthetics and sophistication have doubtless contributed to the company's international success. You won't know where to turn when you find yourself surrounded by all these soaps, shower gels, and mulberry, currant or passion-fruit bath oils. Even more distracting, you will discover the Cucina line and its irresistible washing-up liquid (Sicilian ginger lemon) and the ArtHome range of air fresheners for the house, with mint-lavender aroma (about $24 for a small box of six products). In addition, the store is spacious and the atmosphere convivial.

MAC

3487, bd Saint-Laurent
M° Sherbrooke
☎ (514) 287 9297
www.maccosmetics.com
Mon.-Wed. 10am-7pm,
Thu.-Fri. 10am-9pm,
Sat. 11am-6pm,
Sun. noon-6pm.

Is it still necessary to praise the qualities of this brand of cosmetics? Created in Toronto in 1984 from the brainwave of two professional make-up artists who wanted to market products specifically tailored to their métier, MAC offers a palette of lipsticks and an exceptional choice of eye shadow! You will also find a multitude of hair-brushes and make-up brushes, as well as conditioning creams.

GOAT'S MILK

Surprising as it seems, goat's milk is a great moisturizer. Why? It contains lactic acid, one of the natural components of the skin. And when it's lacking, the skin dries up. In Quebec, they've known that for a long time, and you'll find cosmetics based on goat's milk on every street corner. The most widespread is the soap of the Canus brand, sold in every pharmacy.

Aveda

880, rue Sainte-Catherine Ouest . M° Peel or McGill
☎ (514) 868 1414
www.aveda.com
Mon.-Tue. 10am-6pm, Wed.-Fri. 10am-9pm, Sat. 10am-5pm, Sun. noon-5pm.

To combine beauty with well-being and respect for the environment is the wish of Aveda. In this downtown

boutique-salon, you will find the celebrated hair care that has made the name of this American brand. There is a remarkable line of essential oils of mint and rosemary and diverse shampoos specially developed to safeguard dyed hair.

Bella Pella

3933, rue Saint-Denis
M° Sherbrooke
☎ (514) 845 7328
www.bellapella.com
Mon.-Wed. 11am-6pm, Thu.-Fri. 11am-9pm, Sat. 11am-5pm, Sun. noon-5pm.

Behind the Italian-sounding name, this small Montreal business artistically creates "food" for the skin, combining aromatherapy, culinary art, scientific research and medicinal herbs. The boutique, located in the basement, even has the atmosphere of a laboratory. Its products, of an exceptional fragrance (rose and cardamom, cucumber and aloe, honey and oats, patchouli and orange) leave the skin silky. A practical suggestion: Buy some of the small bars of shampoo for slipping easily into your hand luggage (about $5).

Lise Watier Institut

392, av Laurier Ouest
M° Laurier
☎ (514) 270 9296
www.lisewatier.com
Mon. 9am-5pm, Tue.-Wed. 9am-6pm, Thu.-Fri. 9am-9pm, Sat. 8am-5pm, Sun. 10am-5pm.

A big name in Canadian cosmetics, Lise Watier offers a wide range of makeup, treatments and perfumes – 350 products in all. Its symbol is without doubt the perfume Neiges (Snows), which holds a sales record in Quebec. Among the other flagship products of the company are Hydra City beauty cream, Base Miracle skin cream and the Quatuor line composed of four eye shadows in a little box. And while you're here in the institute, why not have some treatment?

Dans un Jardin

Complexe Desjardins
150, rue Sainte-Catherine Ouest. M° Place-des-Arts
☎ (514) 847 9373
www.dansunjardin.com
Mon.-Wed. 9.30am-6pm, Thu.-Fri. 9.30am-9pm, Sat. 9.30am-5pm, Sun. noon-5pm.

This is a chain of Québécois perfumeries that creates unexpected aromas and flaunts bright colors. Look out for the Coccinelle line, which is not shy about adding a touch of fluorescence to its products. The classic lines, with a fruit or flower base, are delicately aromatic. As for the men, they can spoil themselves with a shower gel smelling of *têtes de violins* ("fiddleheads," or fern roots). As if all that weren't enough, they also sell culinary products.

Art galleries

You can't walk around the streets of Montreal without coming across a host of art galleries. Many of them are concentrated in Vieux-Montréal, in the heart of the Belgo building (see p. 125) or on Rue Sherbrooke, near the Musée des Beaux-Arts. Whatever your feeling about art, these cradles of creativity will fascinate you. There's one for every taste. Here's a small appetizer.

Galerie Elena Lee

1460, rue Sherbrooke Ouest
M° Guy-Concordia
☎ (514) 844 6009
www.galerieelenalee.com
Mar.-Fri. 11am-6pm,
Sat. 11am-5pm.

This gallery, established in 1976, specializes in contemporary glass art. It displays the work of about sixty artists, most of them Canadian, and organizes monthly exhibitions. Several techniques are used, such as ground crystal, thermally molded glass, glassblowing (sometimes shaped with a blowtorch) and glass cast in sand. Don't miss the very beautiful sculptures of Kevin Lockau.

CENTRE DE CÉRAMIQUE BONSECOURS

Ceramics is an art practiced widely in Montreal, and the city harbors a multitude of highly talented artists. The Bonsecours Center is a training college at the heart of which, on the first floor, the work of pupils and of ceramicists already qualified is displayed throughout the year. Teapots, vases and decorative objects of a surprising individuality will captivate you.

444, rue Saint-Gabriel
M° Champ-de-Mars or Place-d'Armes
☎ (514) 866 6581
www.centreceramique bonsecours.net
Mid Jul. to end Aug.: Wed.-Sat. 10.30am-5pm; rest of year: Mon.-Fri. 10am-5pm, Sat. 10.30am-5pm.

Galerie Berensen

1472, rue Sherbrooke Ouest . M° Guy-Concordia
☎ (514) 932 1319
www.galerieberensen.com
Mar.-Fri. 10am-6pm, Sat. 10am-5pm.

Located in a building dating from the early 20th century, this splendid space, graced with high ceilings and immense windows, could only contain an art gallery. Specializing in the paintings, sculpture and photography of contemporary artists, the Berensen Gallery mounts stunning exhibitions, such as the pottery of Picasso, or the fascinating and colorful work of Montreal artist Marc-Aurél Fortier.

Galerie Le Chariot

446, place Jacques-Cartier . M° Champ-de-Mars
☎ (514) 875 4994
www.galerielechariot.com
Mon.-Sat. 10am-6pm, Sun. 10am-3pm.

Considered one of the most important galleries devoted to Inuit works, the Chariot houses some splendid items of all sizes. You will find mainly works in Inukjiak soapstone, snake carvings from Baffin Island and basalt pieces from the Keewatin region. Also fascinating are those carved in whalebone, bear jawbones and walrus skulls.

Galerie M.I.L.K images

133, rue de la Commune Ouest . M° Place-d'Armes
☎ (514) 288 5777
www.milkimages.com
Summer: Tue.-Wed. 10am-6pm, Thu.-Fri. 10am-8pm, Sat. 10am-10pm, Sun. 10am-6pm. Variable hours in winter; inquire.

A little space perfectly located – opposite Montreal's Old Port – the M.I.L.K. Gallery, which displays the work of photographer Ladislas Kadyszewski. After a journey to South Africa, the artist had the bright idea of setting up his own exhibition center devoted to themes emerging from his trip. His black and white and color images are startling in their realism. Great photography.

Galerie Noel Guyomarc'h Bijoux d'Art

137, av. Laurier Ouest
M° Laurier
☎ (514) 840 9362
Mar.-Wed. 11am-6pm, Thu.-Fri. 11am-7.30pm, Sat. 11am-5pm, Sun. noon-5pm.

On first appearance, this gallery is clearly not a goldmine. It seems dark and cramped, its front window is minuscule. But don't go by your first impression: the display is worth the detour. Contemporary works of twenty or so contemporary jewelry artists are displayed here, and the abundance of creativity is striking. The most way-out and unusual materials are deployed, with original and sophisticated results.

Galerie Mazarine

1448, rue Sherbrooke Ouest
M° Guy-Concordia
☎ (514) 982 6566
www.galeriemazarine.com
Mar.-Fri. 10am-6pm, Sat. 10am-5pm.

For those fascinated by the Far East, here is a gallery specializing in Japanese tapestries and prints and Buddhist sculptures – in stone, bronze or wood, coming from Tibet, China and Southeast Asia. You will also find a vast collection of European and American engravings from the 16th through the 19th centuries. In brief, a very specialized outlet that enthusiasts will be glad they found.

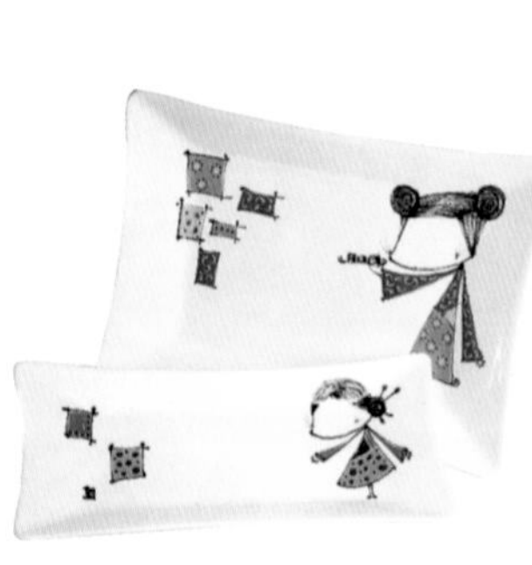

For the home

Montreal offers a plethora of stores devoted to the home, a sphere in which the city is very strong. Many gadgets and accessories, as well as numerous design furniture stores, are gathered along Boulevard saint-Laurent, between Rue Duluth and Avenue Mont-Royal. If interior décor is your passion, you'll love the districts of Westmount, Outremont and Plateau, not forgetting the antique quarter (see p. 69). Keep your eyes open!

Casa

1101, av. Laurier Ouest
M° Laurier, bus 51 or 129
☎ (514) 279 7999
Mon.-Wed. 10am-6pm, Thu.-Fri. 10am-9pm, Sat. 9.30am-5pm, Sun. noon-5pm.

Located right at the end of Avenue Laurier in the Outremont district, Casa is a tasteful and elegant shop offering a quantity of sophisticated objects in which attention has been paid to detail: picture frames, wicker boxes, kitchen utensils, cushions, table sets, china, as well as some magnificent candelabras (about $70). More trivial, but not to be missed, are the extravagant culinary products of the Wildly Delicious brand.

Bleu Nuit

3913, rue Saint-Denis
M° Sherbrooke
☎ (514) 843 9418
www.bleunuit.ca
Mon.-Wed. 10am-6pm, Thu.-Fri. 10am-9pm, Sat. 10am-5.30pm.

Faced with a name like this (Blue Night), one is a bit suspicious. But Bleu Nuit devotes itself to household linen. Cloth of very fine quality covered with serenity-inducing designs is featured in all the collections. It sells top of the range items for bedroom and bathroom with some great bathrobes combining utility and decoration. And to ensure that all is in perfect harmony, beauty products and associated accessories dominate the centre of the store.

Chez Farfelu Maison

838, av. du Mont-Royal Est
M° Mont-Royal
☎ (514) 528 8842
Mon.-Wed. 10am-6pm, Thu.-Fri. 10am-9pm, Sat. 10am-5pm, Sun. 11am-5pm.

This is a paradise of gadgetry, color and fantasy. The tiny boutique is chockful of the little objects that transform a room into a private world: an amusing selection of shower curtains, the zany creations of Alessi, the whacky sponge trays from Koizol of Germany and, especially, the hand-painted crockery of Québécois artists Ketto Design (the sushi dishes are fabulous). No matter how old (or young) you are, you will enjoy this store.

Capharnaüm

1556, av. du Mont-Royal Est
M° Mont-Royal
☎ (514) 525 8900
Mon.-Wed. 11am-6pm, Thu.-Fri. 11am-9pm, Sat. 11am-5pm, Sun. noon-5pm.

A minuscule boutique that is a must for lovers of wooden objects from South Asia and the Far East. From India come carved wooden frames, textiles, tablecloths and cushion covers, as well as wooden furniture, chests and candlesticks. A profusion of ornamental objects at prices that beat all competition. And, to finish with, a wonderful choice of imported incense to perfume your own enchanted evenings.

Arthur Quentin

3960, rue Saint-Denis
M° Sherbrooke
☎ (514) 843 7513
www.arthurquentin.com
Mon.-Wed. 10am-6pm, Thu.-Fri. 10am-9pm, Sat. 10am-5.30pm.

For more than 25 years, Arthur Quentin has been bringing an artistic flair to the task of laying the table. In this store, elegance rather than fantasy sets the tone. You'll find all you desire in the way of dishes, glasses, kitchen utensils, tablecloths and decorative objects – the highest quality, if you require it. It's now or never if you want to buy such practical items as a Japanese grater or a pair of tweezers for removing fish bones.

Vie de Campagne

361, av. Victoria,
M° Vendôme
☎ (514) 484 2199
Mon.-Wed. 10am-5.30pm, Thu.-Fri. 10am-6pm, Sat. 10am-5pm.

In Quebec, nature forms part of the decor: a fact that this boutique, with its rustic furniture, its wooden floor and its quilted bedcovers piled high on shelves, will bring home to you. It exudes an Anglo-Saxon charm reminiscent of our grand-parents' attics! Now is your chance to get something for the garden; or a tea box, a sugar pot or a lovely wooden bird-table.

ZONE

Eye-catching, aesthetically pleasing household items, laid out in a magnificent loft. You won't be able to resist buying some of these distinctive and inexpensive objects. According to your taste, you might go for this set of six aperitif glasses in blown glass, in different shapes and colors, or that adorable tray of artificial flowers and cut herbs; unless you prefer that tiny plastic goldfish, so placid in his aquarium.

5014, rue Sherbrooke Ouest
M° Vendôme
☎ (514) 489 8901
www.zonemaison.com
Mon.-Wed. 10am-6pm, Thu.-Fri. 10am-9pm, Sat. 10am-5.30pm, Sun. 10am-5pm.

Food and drink

You cannot ignore the delicious aromas that waft from Montreal kitchens. Even the famous chefs don't think twice about skillfully mixing conflicting flavors. On the other hand, the produce of the Quebec land is surprisingly delicate; and vegetable, fruit and cheese lovers will have a field day. A word of advice: forget your diet for the time being.

La Tomate

4347, rue de la Roche
M° Mont-Royal
☎ (514) 523 0222
www.tomateonline.com
Wed.-Fri. noon-8pm,
Sat.-Sun. 11am-6pm.

This is an unusual store, offering a range of foodstuffs, all with a tomato base. It's worth trying products such as yellow tomato and maple butter, tomato and apple spread, tomato and red pepper coulis, tomato sauce and pastis, or even tomato sauce with spinach and mandarin. In jars or tubes, these concoctions are surprisingly appetizing.

Le Fromentier

1375, av Laurier Est
M° Laurier
☎ (514) 527 3327

Tue.-Wed. 7am-7pm,
Thu.-Fri. 7am-8pm,
Sat. 7am-6pm,
Sun. 7am-5pm.

You have to pass the railings and descend the stairway to discover this so-called "bread workshop," the only one of its kind. Behind its counter, the dedicated "fromentier" (or "wheat artisan") will take the time to tell you the story of his organic bread and cakes. Exquisite aromas emanate from his *baluchons* (small loaves) stuffed with goat's cheese and spinach, his honeyed-wheat croissants and his treasure trove of special breads. Right next door, the cheese and charcuterie merchants are waiting to receive you. Enjoy your food!

Rachelle-Béry

505, rue Rachel Est
M° Mont-Royal
☎ (514) 524 0725
www.rachellebery.com
Mon.-Tue. 9am-7pm, Wed.-Fri. 9am-9pm, Sat. 9am-6pm, Sun. 10am-6pm.

Highly reputed in Montreal, Rachelle-Béry is a chain of health food stores selling natural and biological foodstuffs. This is the perfect occasion to sample the regional expertise in this sort of food. Those with a sweet tooth will rejoice in the honeys and jams, while others will be tempted by the cheeses and local specialties, like the ketchups - home-made sauces with a fruit and vegetable base to go with meat (nothing to do with Mr Heinz, that's for sure!)

Chocolats Geneviève Grandbois

162, rue Saint-Viateur Ouest . M° Outremont or Laurier, bus 46
☎ (514) 394 1000
www.chocolatsgg.com
Sam.-Wed. 10am-6pm, Thu.-Fri. 10am-9pm.

Skillfully prepared on a foundation of black chocolate, without added sugar, the chocolates of Geneviève Grandbois melt in the mouth in a bold mix of flavors: lavender, pimento, star anise, bergamot orange, maple or olive oil are blended with cocoa. Among the specialties are Chai, an infusion of black Indian tea, ginger, black pepper, star anise, cardamom and...chocolate, of course! Beyond praise.

St-Viateur Bagel

263, rue Saint-Viateur Ouest
M° Outremont or bus no. 46
☎ (514) 276 8044
www.stviateurbagel.com
Mon.-Sun. 24 hours.

At the heart of the Jewish quarter of Outremont, this artisanal bakery makes the most sought-after bagels in Montreal. Here you can watch the cooks extract the bagels from the wood stove by means of an immense spatula. Whether natural, or flavored with sesame seeds or with raisins and cinnamon, they are served very warm. If you prefer to eat them as sandwiches, go to the café located at 1127 av du Mont-Royal Est. And to exercise your taste buds some more, drop into Fairmount (see p. 63).

SAQ

501, place d'Armes
M° Place-d'Armes
☎ (514) 282 4533
Mon.-Wed. and Sat. 10am-6pm, Thu.-Fri. 10am-9pm, Sun. noon-5pm
1108, rue Sainte-Catherine Ouest. M° Peel
☎ (514) 861 7908
Mon.-Sun. 11am-10pm.

SAQ is the government organization that supervises the selling of alcohol. In short, if you want to buy a bottle of champagne, to SAQ you will have to go. Quebec is not noted for its alcoholic products, yet it produces some startling beverages, such as hydromel (honey wine) and cider ice cream. To be consumed in moderation.

PRODUCTS OF THE MAPLE

In Quebec, the taste of maple naturally plays a part in many recipes and ingredients. Gourmands, then, can ingest it at any time of the day. Butter, mustard, salad dressing, tea, ice cream, cakes: all have a touch of the maple about them! Even whisky liqueur is mixed with it to produce a velvety drink called Sortilège (witchcraft). To shop, here are two essential addresses: Les Délices de l'Érable (see p. 99) and Le Marché des Saveurs du Québec (see p. 60).

Shopping malls and department stores

You can't escape them! Shopping malls and department stores form an integral part of the city's urban landscape. Connected to each other by a network of underground galleries (see p. 28), they will tempt you to get lost, the more to prolong your pleasure. And in biting cold and battering rain, you will be happy to see them. They're part of Montreal's lifeblood.

Holt Renfrew

1300, rue Sherbrooke Ouest
M° Peel
☎ (514) 842 5111
www.holtrenfrew.com
Mon.-Wed. 10am-6pm, Thu.-Fri. 10am-9pm, Sat. 9.30am-5pm, Sun. noon-5pm.

Opened in 1908, Holt Renfrew quickly gained its reputation, thanks to its collection of furs. Today the store has largely diversified, though it still retains, on the 2nd floor, a huge space devoted to fur products. The 3rd floor offers young, laid-back fashions, with American brands such as Theory and Elie Tahari. The men's section is on the 1st floor, while the basement houses a chic designer café where you can have a snack of salad or sandwiches.

Simons

977, rue Sainte-Catherine Ouest
M° Peel or McGill
☎ (514) 282 1840
www.simons.com
Mon.-Wed. 10am-7pm, Thu.-Fri. 10am-9pm, Sat. 9.30am-5pm, Sun. noon-5pm.

Founded in Quebec City in 1840, and considered an absolute empire of fashion, the house of Simons did not put down roots in Montreal until 1999. This huge store of three stories sells clothing, household linen and lingerie, offering excellent value for money. In the center of the building, a gigantic sculpture in glass panels, laminated and colored, the work of Guido Molinari, gives the place a distinctive character.

LES COURS MONT-ROYAL

This is unquestionably one of the finest shopping malls in Montreal. Installed in the premises of the former Mont-Royal Hotel – constructed in 1922 and considered at the time to be the biggest such building in the British Empire the mall enjoys an exceptional interior architecture. Natural light illuminates the central court, bringing the best out of its gold, white and gray setting. An impressive chandelier looms above a podium used as a catwalk for fashion parades, while sculptured angels fly through the air.

1455, rue Peel
M° Peel
☎ (514) 842 7777
Mon.-Wed. 10am-6pm, Thu.-Fri. 10am-9pm, Sat. 10am-5pm, Sun. noon-5pm.

Complexe les Ailes

677, rue Sainte-Catherine Ouest
M° McGill
☎ (514) 288 3759
www.complexelesailes.com
Mon.-Wed. 10am-6pm, Thu.-Fri. 10am-9pm, Sat. 9am-5pm, Sun. noon-5pm.

The design of the honey-combed interior, using wood and maroon Plexiglas, gives a 1970s air to this complex, though it was built much more recently than it appears. Undemonstrative and elegant, it houses chic boutiques like La Boutique Sérénité, M0851 (see p. 54) and SAQ Signature. But it's especially to Les Ailes de la Mode, a chain of Montreal department stores, that the local people flock in their thousands.

Centre Eaton

705, rue Sainte-Catherine Ouest; M° McGill
☎ (514) 288 3759
www.centreeatondemontreal.com
Mon.-Fri. 10am-9pm, Sat. 10am-5pm, Sun. noon-5pm.

With more than 175 boutiques and restaurants, as well as six movie theaters, the Eaton Center is definitely the most frequented and the noisiest of the region's shopping malls. Most of the big American chains congregate around here (Gap, Jacob, Levi's, Aldo, Tristan & America). The interior design of the store does not display the originality of its neighbors, but an immense glass roof, allowing the entrance of natural light, makes it nonetheless very agreeable.

La Baie

585, rue Sainte-Catherine Ouest
M° McGill
☎ (514) 281 4422
www.labaie.com
Mon.-Wed. 9.30am-7pm, Thu.-Fri. 9.30am-9pm, Sat. 8am-5pm, Sun. 10am-5pm.

This store of many floors belongs to the Hudson's Bay Company, the oldest commercial firm and the most important chain of retail stores in Canada. You will find sections that are fashionable, cool and inexpensive, as well as a vast beauty department, located on the first floor, offering an array of products based on goat's milk (see p. 113). The section devoted to the home sells a large quantity of decorative objects as well as everyday items of very original design.

Place Montréal Trust

1500, av. McGill College
M° McGill or Peel
☎ (514) 843 8000
www.placemontrealtrust.com
Mon.-Wed. 10am-6pm, Thu.-Fri. 10am-9pm, Sat. 10am-5pm, Sun. noon-5pm.

Place Montréal Trust is smaller than its rival squares, but its interior, a fantasia of color, merits more than a passing glance. An enormous illuminated fountain, installed in the middle, orchestrates the spectacle! The boutiques focus on fashions and accessories, but there is also a large sports area in Le Super Monde des Athlètes, as well as two floors devoted to Indigo's bookstore which stocks both French and English publications.

Gifts
and souvenirs

What could be more uplifting than to take back a distinctive object that will revive memories of your vacation? Whether you're keen on books, ornaments, fashions, jewelry, or whatever else, local handicrafts are one of the best ways of satisfying this desire. Wouldn't they provide a more personal memento than a souvenir sporting a maple leaf?

L'empreinte Coopérative

272, rue Saint-Paul Est
M° Champ-de-Mars
☎ (514) 861 4427
Mon.-Sun. 10am-10pm.

This gallery-boutique sells the works of more than 70 of the best craftspeople in Quebec, from all branches of the arts. You will find whimsical objects, like the papier-mâché napkin rings in the shape of animals, or more serious items such as the splendid ceramic pitchers, or typical souvenirs like the musical wooden spoons (about $22). And in winter they have startling collections of slippers and hats!

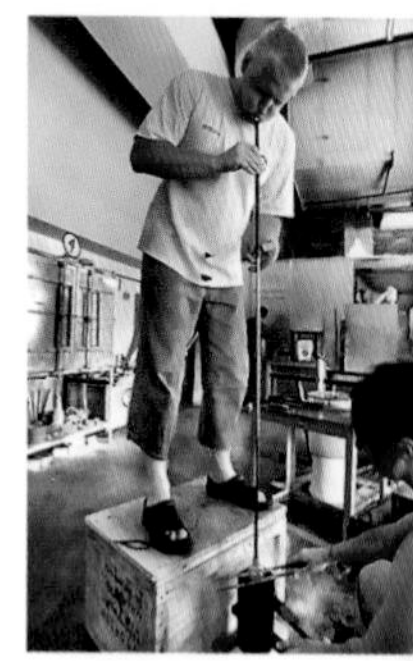

Gogo Glass

Marché Bonsecours
385, rue de la Commune Est
M° Champ-de-Mars
☎ (514) 397 8882 or (514) 878 9698
Hours vary; inquire.

Located on the lower floor of Marché Bonsecours (see p. 41) Gogo Glass is a glassblowing workshop-boutique. You will be able to see the glassblowers at work and to buy some unique examples of dazzling originality. Among these are ne sophisticated two-toned creations of Québec artist nnie Michaud, whose wine lasses, butter dishes and, yes, nortars are irresistible.

Boutique de Pointe-à-Callière

50, rue Saint-Paul Ouest
M° Place-d'Armes
☎ (514) 872 9149
www.pacmusee.qc.ca
nd Jun. to end Aug., Mon.-Sun. 11am-7pm; est of the year, Tue.-Sun. 1am-6pm.

Housed in a historic building, a former customs office, the outique of the Musée de Pointe-à-Callière sells pieces of Native American art, as well as works of historical and archeological interest, a fine collection of stones, articles of pottery and a election of ornamental objects from around the world, including some very pretty sandstone pieces from Africa. There is also a wide choice of crafted jewelry.

Poterie Manu Reva

5141, bd Saint-Laurent
M° Laurier
☎ (514) 948 1717
www.poteriemanureva.com
Mar.-Fri. 10am-6pm, Sat. 10am-5pm.

More than 30 regional ceramic artists are represented in this small boutique behind a blue store-front. The earthenware bread-warmers by Ghislaine Décary are ranged alongside the hunched bodies of Marie-Anne Marchand, the rural creations of Claudel Hêbert, the brush holders of Christian Houle and the ultramodern coffee set designed by Géraldine Sempol. A ceramic serendipity!

L'art des Artisans du Québec

Complexe Desjardins
150, rue Sainte-Catherine Ouest
M° Place-des-Arts
☎ (514) 288 5379
Mon.-Wed. 9.30am-6pm, Thu.-Fri. 9.30am-9pm, Sat. 9.30am-5pm, Sun. noon-5pm.

When you cross the threshold of this boutique you can cast your eye over its wealth of objects, as trivial as they are indispensable. Here you will find the perfect gifts to slip into your suitcase: the little brainwaves from Gabrielle (design rings enabling you to recognize your wine glass!), or the vessels from Léa, decorated with naive figures (about $15 for a whisky glass). Look also at the surprising jewelry items, such as the creations in paper and resin from the Chabert workshop.

Dix Mille Villages

4282, rue Saint-Denis
M° Mont-Royal
☎ (514) 848 0538
www.tenthousandvillages.com
Mon.-Thu. and Sat. 10am-9pm, Fri. 10am-10pm, Sun. 10am-6pm.

Dix Mille Villages (Ten Thousand Villages) is a not-for-profit organization that distributes the work of artists who have come to the country from the developing world. In a friendly atmosphere, you can buy an Indian table, Vietnamese pottery or Peruvian shawls. A small counter serves homemade cakes and fair trade coffee: a good way of combining the pleasant and the useful.

THE ECONOMUSEUMS

This network of enterprises and artisans welcomes you to their respective workshop-boutiques to show you something of their working practices. They use authentic know-how in a effort to preserve indigenous crafts that are unknown or undervalued by the public at large.

La Tranchefile (bookbinding):
5251, bd St-Laurent, ☎ (514) 270 9313.
Les Brodeuses (embroidery):
5364, bd St-Laurent, ☎ (514) 276 4181.
Jules Saint-Michel (lute-making):
57, rue Ontario Ouest, ☎ (514) 288 4343.
Galerie Parchemine (framing):
40, rue Saint-Paul Ouest, ☎ (514) 845 3368.
Tommy Zen (ceramics) :
2261, av Papineau, ☎ (514) 526 6919.

Books, music and cinema

There is plenty to see, read and hear in the Montreal metropolis. And, since you are in a French-speaking city, take advantage of it! Learn about Montreal working-class life through the writings of Michel Tremblay, get hold of the cult movies of Jean-Claude Luzon, or allow yourself to be lulled by the lyric poetry of Richard Desjardins.

Archambault

500, rue Sainte-Catherine Est
M° Berri-UQAM
☎ (514) 849 6201
www.archambault.ca
Mon.-Fri. 9.30am-9pm, Sat. 9am-5pm, Sun. 10am-5pm.

Founded in 1896, Archambault is the best-known music shop in Montreal. Famous for its shelves of jazz and classical music, it is equally well stocked with rock and pop, allowing you to discover the local scene. Musicians themselves are not ignored, with a vast space devoted to instruments.

For those who prefer to watch movies, the DVD selection is very interesting. It's your opportunity to get hold of some Canadian TV series or cult movies.

Future Shop

470, rue Sainte-Catherine Ouest
M° Place-des-Arts
☎ (514) 393 2600
www.futureshop.ca
Mon.-Fri. 10am-9pm, Sat. 9am-5pm, Sun. 10am-5pm.

To listen to your favorite music any time of the day, you need to be well equipped. At Future Shop, a run-of-the-mill store dedicated to the sale of electronic equipment, you will find a wide choice of Discmans and MP3 players – including the ubiquitous iPod. There are also attractive deals on digital cameras and camcorders.

DVD Passion

Centre Eaton
705, rue Sainte-Catherine Ouest
M° McGill
☎ (514) 845 2929
Mon.-Fri. 10am-9pm, Sat. 10am-5pm, Sun. noon-5pm.

As its name indicates, this store is aimed at DVD enthusiasts. The premises are not very big,

but the choice is interestingly diverse. Remember that if you are traveling from outside North America, DVDs bought in Canada correspond to zone 1. Special offers and boxed sets allow you to pick up some bargains.

Librairie Renaud-Bray

1432, rue Sainte-Catherine Ouest
M° Guy-Concordia
☎ (514) 876 9119
www.renaud-bray.com
Mon.-Wed. 10am-6pm, Thu.-Fri. 10am-9pm, Sat. 9am-5pm, Sun. noon-5pm.

The Renaud-Bray bookstore chain is the best place to start looking for novels and books of all kinds, as well as music and DVDs. It also offers you the chance to become better acquainted with the riches of Québécois and Canadian literature. This store stocks a range of modern Canadian literature in the English language, some originally written in English and some translations of Québécois French novels.

Librairie ABC Livres d'art

Édifice Belgo
372, rue Sainte-Catherine Ouest
M° Place-des-Arts
☎ (514) 878 9205
www.ABCartbookscanada.com
Tue.-Sat. 11am-6pm.

Located on the first floor of the Belgo building – which houses many contemporary art galleries – the ABC Bookstore is an excellent place for lovers of art books. There are magnificent works on painting, sculpture and

photography, as well as fine volumes of art history and criticism, and books devoted to young contemporary artists. Although many are in French, you will also find some English titles. And if your French is a bit rusty, you can always look at the pictures!

Indigo

Place Montréal Trust
1500, av. McGill Collège
M° Peel or McGill
☎ (514) 281 5549
www.chapters.indigo.ca
Mon.-Wed. 10am-6pm, Thu.-Fri. 10am-9pm, Sat. 10am-5pm, Sun. noon-5pm.

Indigo could be seen as the big rival of the Renaud-Bray bookstores, except that the majority of the titles are English literature. Whether you're looking to pick up a copy of a Shakespeare play or an English children's comic book, this is the place to look. There is a wide selection of books of all sorts, from literary classics to popular novels and non-fiction, as well as children's books, magazines, gifts and an upstairs café in which you can browse through your selection before buying.

BOOKSTORE OF THE CANADIAN CENTER FOR ARCHITECTURE (CCA)

Modern architecture, town planning, history and theory of architecture, photography, landscape and garden architecture, heritage conservation, museology (museum management) and design around the world: these are some of the themes covered by this superbly stocked bookstore, which is well worth a visit. The works are accessible and very interesting. What better way to discover the history of a city than to study the history of its buildings?

1920, rue Baile
M° Guy-Concordia or Atwater
☎ (514) 939 7028
Tue.-Sun. 11am-6pm, Thu. 11am-9pm.

Some curiosities

Targeted at collectors and lovers of the unusual, these specialist stores offer journeys into other worlds. The medieval period predominates, with a quantity of shops devoted to its clothing and traditions. This is the time to pick up that fun gift for your oldest friend!

Excalibor

122, rue Saint-Paul Est
M° Place-d'Armes
☎ (514) 393 7260
Sun.-Wed. 11am-9pm, Thu.-Sat. 11am-10pm.

Have you ever wanted to dress up in cape and sword, or wear a suit of armor? You can easily do it, thanks to the Excalibor boutique. A grand choice of accessories and costumes from the medieval period, created by a team of Québécois designers, is offered you. The salespeople, wearing the traditional gear, expound enthusiastically on the merits of their goods. And if this style seems a bit over the top to you, you can always buy a gargoyle instead! This store is lots of fun, even if you are just looking.

Chez Farfelu Curiosités

843, av. du Mont-Royal Est
M° Mont-Royal
☎ (514) 528 6251
Mon.-Wed. 10am-6pm, Thu.-Fri. 10am-9pm, Sat. 10am-5pm, Sun. 11am-5pm.

The younger relation of Farfelu Maison (see p. 117) is the realm of whimsy and gizmos. Amid dazzling colors, a multitude of objects is piled high on the shelves. From the "Pig Catapult" to the "Nichons Plus" massage oil, there are plenty of things to divert you. Also on sale is a huge selection of postcards.

Noël Éternel

461, rue Saint-Sulpice
M° Place-d'Armes
☎ (514) 285 4944
www.noeleternel.com
Mon.-Wed. 9am-6pm, Thu.-Sun. 9am-8pm.

To keep Christmas going the whole year through, this magical store offers a multitude of decorations, miniatures and other accessories, some flashier than others.

You will also find amusing novelties, like an electric Santa Claus doing stomach exercises, and the gorgeous fairy godmothers made by Jacqueline Kent (about $50). There are also some splendid Nativities for the purists, and a homemade fudge – a sort of delicious little brownie – especially for gourmands.

Le Châtelet des Chevaleries Sacrées

919, av Laurier Est
M° Laurier
☎ (514) 279 9312
Mon.-Wed. 10am-6pm, Thu.-Fri. 10am-9pm, Sat. 10am-5pm.

This temple of the esoteric and the medieval is one of the principal curiosities in Montreal. Here there

are no garments: only jewels, talismans, objects of ritual and magic. Among these are the irresistible *diablotins* (imps; about $7), the garden "groms" and some lovely candlesticks in the shape of gargoyles. But the chief attraction is the incredible collection of traditional incense (sold in powder, not in sticks). If you ask the proprietor about the history and quality of each one, you'll be there all day.

La Boutique du Grand Prix

161, rue Saint-Paul Est
M° Champ-de-Mars
☎ (514) 392 1212
www.boutiquedugrandprix.com
Mon.-Sun. 10am-midnight.

Formula 1 fans will be mesmerized. Each year, Montreal hosts the Canadian Grand Prix on its Gilles Villeneuve track (see p. 73). In this store you will find accessories, clothing and gadgets bearing the logos of the different racing teams, as well as a fine selection of models.

Pause Rétro

2054, rue Saint-Denis
M° Sherbrooke
☎ (514) 848 0333
Mon.-Tue. 11am-6.30pm, Thu.-Fri. 11am-9.30pm, Sat. 11am-7.30pm, Sun. noon-5.30pm.

Bar decorations, neon signs, advertisements, street nameplates, old gas-pumps, not to mention the huge collection of bric-a-brac linked to the Coca-Cola brand-name: whether you are a serious collector or simply feeling nostalgic for the 1950s or 60s, you will surely find something here to take home with you.

AU PAPIER JAPONAIS

This store stocks everything to do with Japanese paper art. As soft as cloth and as beautiful as a painting, these papers will delight you. You will discover the different components of this art, and particularly its motifs: Chiyogami, Obonai and Kyo-Komon. Some of the boutique's creations – purses, tea boxes and a variety of notebooks and address books – have even been made from this paper. And don't miss the lamp collection in the second room.

24, av Fairmount Ouest
M° Laurier
☎ (514) 276 6863
Mon.-Sat. 10am-6pm (Thu. until 9pm), Sun. noon-6pm.

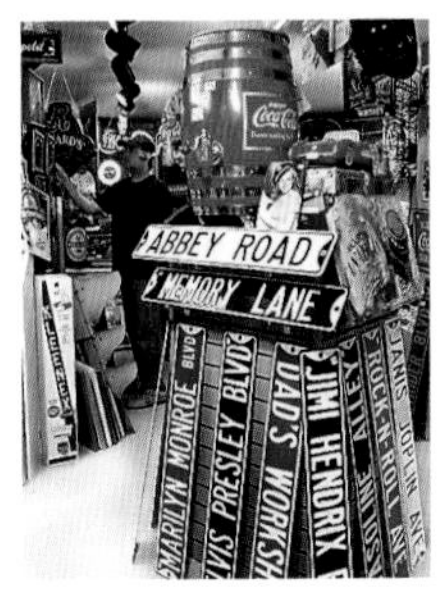

Sports and fresh air

Sport and the joys of the open air form an integral part of Montreal's daily life: cycling, rollerblading and jogging in summer; skiing, squash, and ice skating in winter, not to mention weekend expeditions into untamed nature. As a visitor, you can take advantage of these opportunities. After all, you're on vacation.

Le Yéti

5190, bd Saint-Laurent
M° Laurier
☎ (514) 271 0773
www.leyeti.ca
Mon.-Wed. 10am-6pm,
Thu.-Fri. 10am-9pm,
Sat. 9.30am-5pm,
Sun. noon-5pm.

A little out of the way, this shop is nonetheless a real haven for lovers of mountain-climbing, skiing, skating and cycling. It is set out on two huge floors, where you will find all the best equipment for cross-country skiing, racket sports and downhill skiing, as well as a large area devoted to cycling – with brands such as Bianchi and Fisherbikes. Cycling enthusiasts should know that Le Yéti is also a cycling club.

Boutique Courir

4452, rue Saint-Denis
M° Mont-Royal
☎ (514) 449 9600
www.boutiquecourir.com
Mon.-Wed. 9.30am-6pm,
Thu.-Fri. 9.30am-9pm,
Sat. 9.30am-5pm,
Sun. noon-5pm.

Something of a general store, although, as its name suggests, a large space is devoted to running shoes, you can find, on different levels, a large choice of women's sportswear at very competitive prices. On the first floor, there is a selection of cool and useful accessories, such as Camelbak rucksacks, and Eaglecreek saddlebags for cyclists.

Atmosphère

1610, rue Saint-Denis
M° Berri-UQAM
☎ (514) 844 2228
Mon.-Fri. 10am-9pm, Sat. 10am-5pm, Sun. 11am-5pm.

Installed between Saint Denis Theatre and a cinema complex, this huge store devotes itself to sports and leisure activities in a very friendly ambience – particularly attractive are the colorful kayaks hanging from the ceiling! A camping and hiking area offers practical and functional accessories as well as a good selection of walking boots.

Golf Town

1231, rue Sainte-Catherine Ouest
M° Peel
☎ (514) 848 0078
www.golftown.com
Mon.-Wed. 10am-6pm, Thu.-Fri. 10am-9pm, Sat. 10am-5pm, Sun. 11am-5pm.

Lovers of golf will feel at home in this temple of almost 20,000sq. ft. Golf Town is considered the most important retailer devoted to golf in the whole of Canada, and you would be unlucky not to find the accessory you wanted. Clubs, bags, balls, gloves, clothing, shoes, even a selection of books: equip yourself here, and you'll be that much readier for your next game!

La Maison du Hamac

2009, rue Saint-Denis
M° Berri-UQAM or Sherbrooke
☎ (514) 982 9440
Mon.-Wed. 11am-6pm, Thu.-Fri. 11am-9pm, Sat. 9am-6pm, Sun. noon-6pm.

Minuscule but colorful, this boutique offers a quantity of hammocks from various

Central and South American countries. String or sewn, the hammocks are handmade, and some models come with wooden rods at their ends. It's so easy to slide one of these into your baggage; why hesitate?

Altitude

4140, rue Saint-Denis
M° Mont-Royal
☎ (514) 847 1515
www.altitude-sports.com
Mon.-Wed. 10am-6pm, Thu.-Fri. 10am-9pm, Sat. 10am-5pm, Sun. noon-5pm.

One can't say it often enough: Quebec is paradise for nature lovers. This store, like so many others, has understood this, and so specializes in that domain. Here you will find all you ever wanted for your next hike or camping expedition. And, if you are a keen mountaineer, this is a great place to purchase your equipment.

Underworld

289, rue Sainte-Catherine Est
M° Berri-UQAM
☎ (514) 284 6473
www.underworld-shop.com
Mon.-Wed. and Sat. 10am-6pm, Thu.-Fri. 10am-9pm, Sun. 11am-6pm.

This place is entirely given over to the universe of the skateboard. On the first floor, you'll find ultra-cool garments and accessories (from trainers to pocketbooks); on the second floor, the famous boards, all vying with each other to be the most colorful and creative. It's vital to check out how you look from head to toe, before making a striking appearance on the sidewalks of your favorite skateboarding city.

KANUK

A small Québécois enterprise founded thirty years ago, Kanuk specializes in making warm and insulated coats, to help you survive the harshness of the local winters. Conceived with extreme adventure and winter camping expeditions in mind – but also for getting about town – they are available in many shapes and colors. But be warned: high-tech products come at a price, and you will need to part with about $450 for a waterproof coat.

485, rue Rachel Est
M° Mont-Royal
☎ (514) 284 4494
www.kanuk.com
Mon.-Wed. 9am-6pm, Thu.-Fri. 9am-9pm, Sat. 10am-5pm, Sun. noon-5pm.

Secondhand and discount stores

Most of the secondhand and discount stores are concentrated in the Plateau district and around Avenue du Mont-Royal. End-of-the-line sales have always delighted shopping addicts, while for a younger, less formal generation browsing through secondhand markets constitutes a way of life in itself. So, whatever your preferred style, you'll find something to please you.

Eva B.

2013, bd Saint-Laurent
M° Saint-Laurent
☎ (514) 849 8246
Mon.-Wed. and Sat. 10am-8pm, Thu.-Fri. 10am-9pm, Sun. noon-8pm.

A brilliant concept underlies the design of this boutique: on the right, the part reserved for new garments (already aquiring a casual secondhand aura), and on the left, the real secondhand section, decked out with a retro bar dispensing coffee, ice cream and cakes. Very disarming! And everything is here, from faded jeans to summer frocks, by way of children's tuxedos. You can even hire a suit, if need be, on the second floor. The service is truly charming, and the store has plans to open a gallery. Definitely a place to visit.

L'AUBAINERIE

Its name explains everything. L'Aubainerie (Windfall) is a chain of Quebec stores that offers fashionable clothes for the whole family at the lowest market prices. What mother could resist its ultra-trendy children's T-shirts for under $10? The men's section, especially sportswear, is equally worth a detour, not to mention the alluring accessories: hats, purses, etc.

1490, av. du Mont-Royal Est
M° Mont-Royal
☎ (514) 521 0059
www.aubainerie.com
Mon.-Fri. 9am-9pm, Sat.-Sun. 9am-5pm.

Échantillons Solo

1328, av Laurier Est
M° Laurier
☎ (514) 521 7656
Tue.-Wed. 11am-8pm,
Thu.-Fri. 11am-9pm,
Sat.-Sun. 11am-5pm.

This is a charming local boutique-discount store full of nice surprises. Women are accorded the place of honor, with some magnificent brightly colored dresses and mid-length skirts in exotic patterns. Original brands such as Groovy and Oonu are represented. And, right in the corner of the room, there's a neat collection of jewelry from which to choose the perfect accessory for your outfit.

L'Atelier

4247, rue Saint-André
M° Mont-Royal
Jeu.-Fri. 10am-6pm,
Sat. 10am-5pm.

L'Atelier (Workshop) is a tiny discount store of homemade linen which is full of wonderful things. It sells the outdated collections of Bleu Nuit and Arthur Quentin (see p. 116), so the quality of its products is guaranteed. The prices are very attractive. Pay close attention to the sizes of the sheets, which sometimes differ from their European equivalents ("queen size", for instance, is slightly smaller than it is in Europe).

Folles Alliées

365, av. du Mont-Royal Est
M° Mont-Royal
☎ (514) 843 4904
Mon.-Wed. 11am-6pm,
Thu.-Fri. 11am-9pm, Sat.
11am-5pm, Sun. noon-5pm.

Folles Alliées (Crazy Allies) is the perfect spot for those in search of rare items and old clothes. In a store scarcely bigger than a bedroom, you find leather jackets, retro dresses, pumps, while some superb hats and accessories from the 1930s and 1940s are ranged along the walls and ceilings. It's a happy hunting ground. The fitting room alone, edged with carved wood, is worth the visit.

Jacob Outlet

4268, rue Saint-Denis
M° Mont-Royal
☎ (514) 845 8383
Mon.-Wed. 10am-6pm,
Thu.-Fri. 10am-9pm,
Sat. 10am-5pm,
Sun. noon-5pm.

If you liked the modish, feminine styles of Jacob (see p. 103), and the youth fashions and sportswear of Jacob Connexion (see p. 108), you'll want to make a beeline for the discount store of those two brand-names. Sure, the styles are passé, but when you're making a great deal, that issue doesn't even arise! On this subject, note that shoemakers Aldo (see p. 111) also have a liquidation store (250, rue Sainte-Catherine Est).

Friperie St-Laurent

3976, bd Saint-Laurent
M° Sherbrooke or Mont-Royal
☎ (514) 842 3893
Mon.-Wed. 11am-6pm,
Thu.-Fri. 11am-9pm,
Sat. 11am-5pm,
Sun. noon-5pm.

The highly alluring display windows will no doubt make you want to enter this discount store with its lovely smell of old leather. Coats cost around $85, and you can find various styles of leather jacket from $40. You can find most other things as well, from old Navy T-shirts to bathing suits and "classic" Hawaiian shirts. And don't miss the wonderful accessories, such as the beautiful purses.

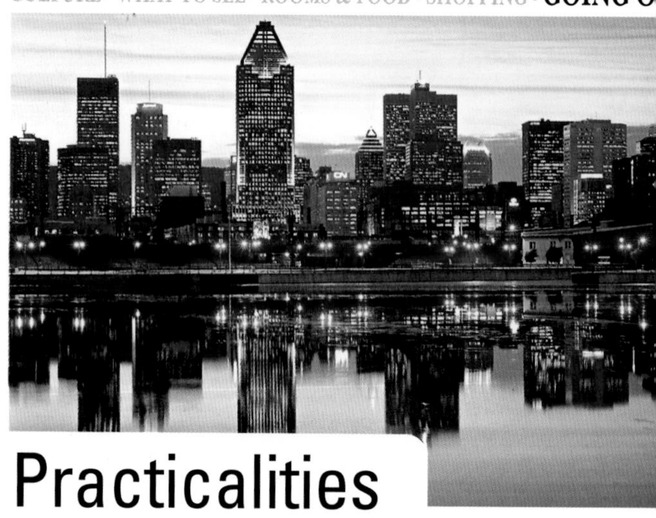

Practicalities

Where to go

Montreal possesses a plethora of bars, theaters and nightclubs which can keep you occupied all night long. In addition, in summer the town lives to the beat of its many festivals. Strategic spots are undoubtedly Boulevard Saint-Laurent for its numerous stylish bars, Rue Crescent for its pubs and its Anglophone ambience, the Latin Quarter and the Plateau for their many theaters, downtown for its nightclubs and maybe the Village for its frenetic nightlife.

Program

The best way to get to know what's going on culturally in the town is to obtain the weeklies *Voir, Ici, Hour* or *Mirror.* They appear on Thursdays and are given out for free on the subway. The first two are in French, the last two in English. You can get the news as well as some deeper articles in the daily *La Presse*. Moreover, the tourist office brings out a quarterly brochure entitled "Quoi faire à Montréal" (What to Do in Montreal), which might give you some ideas.

Buying tickets

You can buy your ticket directly at the box office, but this is not always reliable, given the variable opening hours. To enable you to buy tickets in advance (even from outside Canada), there are networks that distribute tickets for every kind of show or event, even sporting ones. Whether you buy your tickets by phone or through the Internet, you will need to pay by banker's card, and may often need to show this even when you turn up to collect them.

HIGH TIMES

Numerous festivals punctuate the rhythm of the city throughout the year (see p. 20). Among them are the incomparable International Jazz Festival (June and July), Francofolies (July and August), and the Just For Laughs Festival, a multidisciplinary spectacle, with numerous shows, activities and gastronomic adventures.
Sports fans can also follow various tournaments and competitions throughout the year (see p .22). Hockey, football, soccer, tennis or Formula 1: take your pick.

Billetterie de la Place des Arts
Mon.-Sat., noon to 9pm
☎ (866) 842 2112.
Ticketpro
www.ticketpro.ca
☎ (514) 908-9090 or (866) 908 9090
Admission
www.admission.com
☎ (514) 790-1245
(800) 361-4595

Security

Montreal is one of the safest cities in North America. On Rue Sainte-Catherine Est, you may come across young people asking for money, but even if their appearance is a bit startling (in the punk mode) they aren't usually aggressive and won't press the point. So you can amble through the streets at your ease by day or in the evening, and make the most of your long weekend.

Alcohol: opening times and regulations

In general, shows begin at 8pm. Between 5 and 7pm, the bars often feature a "happy hour," an institution much appreciated by Montrealers. The night clubs open their doors at 10pm and close at 3am, like the bars. The uniformity of this closing time is accounted for by a law forbidding the sale of alcohol after three o'clock in the morning. Another law forbids the consumption of alcohol on the street.

Hunger pangs

If, after a show or an evening in a nightclub, you are suddenly seized by ravenous hunger, what can you do? You can always find cafés and convenience stores open 24/24 downtown, on Rue Saint-Denis or in the heart of the Latin Quarter. For a more substantial meal, go to the brasserie Express or the trattoria BU, both of them open until 2am (see p. 94). If you've a craving for smoked meat, head for Ben's Delicatessen (see p. 49) and the crazy bagels of Fairmount (see p. 63). If none of these will do, you can always try the incomparable Club Sandwich. With its air of a 1950s diner, this restaurant, open 24/24, is one of the favorite rendezvous for nighthawks.
Club Sandwich
1570, rue Sainte-Catherine Est, M° Papineau.
☎ (514) 521 1419

FINDING YOUR WAY

You will find details of the nearest metro station (M°) after the address in the Going Out section.

Bars and shows

1 - Le Saint-Sulpice
2 - Altitude 737
3 - Le Cheval Blanc
4 - Le Magellan

Bars

Galerie 1225 Art et Vin

1225, rue de la Montagne
M° Guy-Concordia
☎ (514) 395 1225
Tue.-Fri. 10am-10pm, Saturday 11am-10pm.

Both a bar and an art gallery, this space occupying two floors is the perfect spot to relax with a glass at the start of the evening. The canvases hung on the big stone walls lend a chic and modish air to the place. A new exhibition is displayed every month. The wine list is interesting, and to top it off plates of cheese or foie gras can accompany the wine.

Le Cheval Blanc

809, rue Ontario Est
M° Berri-UQAM
☎ (514) 522 0211
Mon.-Tue. 3pm-1am, Wed.-Sat. 3pm-3am, Sunday 5pm-1am.

Le Cheval Blanc (the White Horse) is one of the oldest micro-breweries of Montreal. In this tiny but friendly, sombe[r] but phantasmagorical plac[e] (with plants climbing u[p] the wall), you drink th[e] two homemade beers, "Ca[p] Tourmente" and "Berlue." Some evenings, a jazz tri[o] participates in the proceedings. The atmosphere is ver[y] friendly.

Dieu du Ciel

29, av Laurier Ouest
M° Laurier
☎ (514) 490 9555
Mon.-Sun. 3pm-3am.

This is another micro-brewery much appreciated by Montrealers. Bigger and noisier than Le Cheval Blanc, this tavern offers a range of subtly flavored

TO SEE AND BE SEEN

Don't miss the incomparable view offered by the ultra-cool Altitude 737 (see p. 47), nor the unpretentious and friendly ambience of Newtown (see p. 51).

artisan beers. Ale lovers will be thoroughly at home here. And it's also possible to eat (pizzas, salads, sandwiches, etc.). Count on spending $4 on a pint before 7pm, and $5.25 thereafter.

Le Saint-Sulpice

1680, rue Saint-Denis
M° Berri-UQAM
☎ (514) 844 9458
Mon.-Sun. 11.30am-3am.

Spread over four floors, this bar-restaurant-nightclub is a high spot in the Latin Quarter. Students from the nearby university are among its most faithful customers, so the scene is rather youthful. Sometimes a group comes to perform here. In summer, this bar is taken by storm, on account of its agreeable garden, located in the rear.

Laïka

4040, bd Saint-Laurent
M° Mont-Royal
☎ (514) 842 8088
Mon.-Fri. 8.30am-3am, Sat.-Sun. 9am-3am.

Here you can take a light meal and coffee throughout the day, but it's really in the evening that the Laïka comes into its own. In the midst of a bright and sophisticated interior, this very fashionable lounge welcomes different DJs for evenings of drum 'n' bass, funk or electro, each of them equally popular.

Le Magellan

330, rue Ontario Est
M° Sherbrooke ou Berri-UQAM
☎ (514) 845 0909
Mon.-Fri. 11am-11pm, Sat.-Sun. 11am-midnight.

With its wooden interior, the Magellan has the air of a pub rather than a bar. The numerous books arranged on the shelves, along with the background music, give a warm, family glow to the place. On the second story, artists occasionally appear or conferences take place. But you can also have a snack there, as many do at weekends.

Concert bars

Café Sarajevo

2080, rue Clark
☎ (514) 284 5629
M° Saint-Laurent
Sun.-Thu. 5pm-1am, Fri.-Sat. 5pm-3am
Admission charge for concerts.

Located near boulevard Saint-Laurent, the Sarajevo café puts on jazz concerts at the end of the evening, as well as *tzigane* (gypsy) music in a delirious atmosphere. It's not unknown for the public to get up and dance! Aside from its concerts, it's a very friendly café where you can drink good wines and eat several Slav specialties.

Hurley's Irish Pub

1225, rue Crescent
M° Guy-Concordia
☎ (514) 861 4111
Mon.-Sun. 11am-3.30am.

This is one of the oldest pubs in Montreal. Ideally located in the heart of Rue Crescent, Hurley's will give you a memorable evening, thanks to its musicians, specialists in Irish folklore! Lovers of scotch and Irish whiskey will have found their niche. The others can always huddle down by the log fire, warmly welcome in winter.

L'Escogriffe

4467A, rue Saint-Denis
M° Mont-Royal
☎ (514) 842 7244
Mon.-Sun. noon-3am
Admission charge for certain events

This place, short on space, soon gets full on concert nights. Jazz dominates the program, with evenings devoted to Django Reinhardt or the Swing Manouche quartet, among others. Rock and jazz-funk are often in full swing. In short, a good place to drink a glass, especially since the excellent beers from local microbreweries are on tap.

Bistro à Jojo

1627, rue Saint-Denis
M° Berri-UQAM
☎ (514) 843 5015
Mon.-Sun. 11am-3am.

Known as the home of the blues, this bar (with pub overtones) welcomes each evening some groups from the local scene, whether they play blues (most of the time) or rock (certain evenings). In summer, the big bay windows, overlooking Rue Saint-Denis, are wide open, allowing the passers-by to enjoy their fill of the music.

Casa del Popolo

4873, bd Saint-Laurent
M° Laurier
☎ (514) 284 3804
Mon. noon-midnight, Wed.-Sun. noon-3am
Admission charge for certain events.

Simultaneously a vegetarian restaurant, a café and a music hall, La Casa del Popolo is a place much frequented by young epicureans and street style freaks. Concerts of all types of music

TAKE A RAIN CHECK

There are many movie theaters in Montreal. Depending on the particular venue, you can watch a movie in the original English or French (with subtitles). For arthouse and independent movies, try Ex-Centris (see p. 55).

take place here, as well as DJ evenings (Mondays) and soirées dedicated to the spoken word. Directly opposite is the second room, the Sala Rossa, where various music events (rock, reggae, Indie, flamenco) happen, as well as a restaurant serving tapas and paella.

Foufounes Électriques

87, rue Sainte-Catherine Est
M° Saint-Laurent
☎ (514) 844 5539
Mon.-Sun. 2pm-3am
Admission charge for concerts.

Legendary haunt of Montreal nightlife, Foufounes (which means "buttocks" in Quebec French) has been promoting evenings of rock, punk, hard rock, gothic and techno for many years. It is at the same time a bar (with a large terrace), a concert hall and a club. Suffice to say that the atmosphere is caustic, the music very loud, and the decor a purist's nightmare, beginning with the exterior façade of the place, which will give you a good foretaste!

Jello Bar

151, rue Ontario Est
☎ (514) 285 2621
M° Saint-Laurent
Tue. et Sat.9pm-3am, Wed.-Fri. 5pm-3am
Admission charge.

The chic retro decoration is absolutely gorgeous and the ambience extremely convivial. Each night the Jello Bar mounts concerts of funk, R & B, salsa or swing. The menu offers more than fifty original and lively cocktails. For those who eschew dancing, there is a pool table at the far end of the room.

House of Jazz

2060, rue Aylmer
M° McGill
☎ (514) 842 8656
Mon.-Wed. 11.30am-12.30am, Thu. 11.30am-1.30am, Fri. 11.30am-2.30am, Sat. 6pm-2.30am, Sun. 6pm-12.30am
Admission charge for some events.

Formerly known under the name of Biddle's (in honor of double bassist Charlie Biddle), House of Jazz, considered the main jazz club of Montreal, welcomes the big names of the Canadian scene. The restaurant specializes in Louisiana dishes: its chicken and chops combination is justly famous.

Upstairs Jazz Club

1254, rue MacKay
M° Guy-Concordia
☎ (514) 931 6808
Mon.-Thu. noon-1am, Fri. noon-3am
Sat. 5pm-3am
Sun. 5pm-1am.

Less touristy than House of Jazz, this club puts on jazz concerts featuring local musicians. Anglophone students flock to it. The Upstairs is also an agreeable, brightly lit café-restaurant, graced with a charming terrace at the back.

1 - Upstairs Jazz Club
2 - Le Magellan
3 - Théâtre du Nouveau Monde
4 - Sky Pub Sky Club

Nightclubs

Funky Town

1454A, rue Peel
M° Peel
☎ (514) 282 8387
Thu.-Sat.10pm-3am
Admission charge (except Thu.).

Its name tells you everything: you are in the kingdom of funk! The luminous checkerboard of the dance floor and the retro armchairs amusingly recall the bygone era of Saturday Night Fever. Thursdays, in general, are given over to French hits of the 1950s, 60s and 70s. You have been warned.

Aria

1280, rue Saint-Denis
M° Berri-UQAM
☎ (514) 987 6712
Fri.-Sat.1.30am-10am
Admission charge.

The answer to every insatiable dance floor addict's (or insomniac's) prayer, the Aria club is the most popular after-hours venue in Montreal. Its three different levels, including of course a techno area, allow you to choose your favorite type of music. In order to minimize the risk of over-

crowding and overindulgence, no alcohol is sold in this establishment.

Newtown

1476, rue Crescent
M° Guy-Concordia
☎ (514) 284 6555
Fri.-Sat.10pm-3am
Admission charge.

At weekends, the clientele, heterogeneous but always chic, crowds into this stylish club, an integral part of the superb Newtown complex (see p. 51). The varied music alternates between funk, pop, R & B, or any sound inciting its hearers to dance and make merry. It is one of the shining beacons on Rue Crescent.

Sky Pub Sky Club

1474, rue Sainte-Catherine Est
M° Beaudry
☎ (514) 529 6969
Mon.-Sun. 11am-3am
Admission charge (except for the pub).

Located in the heart of the Village, the Sky is a complex favored by the gay community. First, there is the pub, largely populated by men, then there is the cabaret, offering transvestite shows, and lastly there is the nightclub. The latter, endowed with several dance floors for different styles of music, caters to a clientele that is festive and on the young side (heterosexuals are welcome). In summer, the roof terrace allows you to make the most of the weather.

Le Diable Vert

4557, rue Saint-Denis
M° Mont-Royal
☎ (514) 849 5888
Mon.-Sun. 5pm-3am
Admission charge.

GESÙ AND LA PLACE DES ARTS

The performance hall of the Gesù creativity center (see p. 53) offers a very rich program, drawn from different worlds and promoting new talent. In a completely different style, the Place des Arts complex (see p. 52), hub of the town's cultural life, is the essential venue for lovers of classical music, ballet and opera.
Information:
Orchestre Symphonique de Montréal :
☎ (514) 84 9951
Grands Ballets Canadiens : ☎ (514) 849 8681
Opéra de Montréal : ☎ (514) 985 2222

With its bright red interior, one wonders why this place is called "The Green Devil"! Aside from that, it's indubitably one of the most popular places in town among 18-25 year olds. It's not a classic nightclub, but rather a bar that happens to have a dance floor. The music shifts between rock, salsa, hip-hop and world music. At weekends, you'll have to exercise patience: the line to get in can be very long!

Club Vatican

1432, rue Crescent
M° Guy-Concordia
☎ (514) 845 3922
Fri.-Sat.10pm-3am
Admission charge.

Located a stone's throw from Newtown, Club Vatican addresses itself to lovers of hip-hop and R & B, with a bias towards techno on Thursdays, house on Fridays and funk on Saturdays. The clientele is varied and the ambience always festive. Comfortable armchairs allow you to relax between dancing feats.

Shows

Théâtre du Nouveau Monde

84, rue Sainte-Catherine Ouest; M° Place-des-Arts
☎ (514) 866 8668
Variable prices, in general between $15 and $50.

After welcoming many and varied companies for over a century, the Theatre of the New World (TNM), renovated in 1997, nowadays only admits classic theatrical works to its repertoire. It thus presents plays by Kafka, Shakespeare, Federico Garcia Lorca and even Nancy Houston.

Théâtre d'Aujourd'hui

3900, rue Saint-Denis
M° Mont-Royal
☎ (514) 282 3900
Prices: from $21 to $26.

The Théâtre d'Aujourd'hui has devoted itself for 35 years to works of Québécois origin. You can enjoy original works by local playwrights, if your French is good enough to follow the gist.

Agora de la Danse

840, rue Cherrier Est
M° Sherbrooke
☎ (514) 525 1500
Prices: from $16 to $25.

Housed in a building of the University of Quebec at Montreal (UQAM), l'Agora de la Danse presents shows of contemporary and experimental dance with artists such as Margie Gills and Harold Rhéaume.

1 - *Bistro à Jojo*
2 - *Opéra de Montréal*
3 - *Bistro à Jojo*
4 - *Foufounes Électriques*

Spectrum

318, rue Sainte-Catherine Ouest
M° Place-des-Arts
☎ (514) 861 5851
Variable prices, in general between $15 and $40.

Housed in a former movie theater, Spectrum is a well-established venue for Montreal soirées. Its charming interior, exuding a dash of retro, has welcomed many multi-disciplinary shows, as well as some of the big names in music, such as Céline Dion, Miles Davis and even Tina Turner. Its program remains very varied, and its hall plays a major role as a venue for the Festival of Jazz.

Théâtre La Chapelle

3700, rue Saint-Dominique
M° Sherbrooke
☎ (514) 843 7738
Variable prices, in general between $15 and $25.

A multidisciplinary room par excellence, Théâtre La Chapelle copes equally well with performances of dance, theater or contemporary music. Its program gives priority to original creations based on research and experimentation.

Théâtre du Rideau Vert

4664, rue Saint-Denis
M° Mont-Royal
☎ (514) 845 0712
Prices vary depending on the show.

The Theatre of the Green Curtain is the doyen of Canadian theaters. Installed on Rue Saint-Denis since 1960, it offers a very varied program, from classic drama to contemporary creations, including musical shows.

Monument National

1182, bd Saint-Laurent
M° Saint-Laurent
☎ (514) 871 2224
Prices vary around $20.

Erected in 1893 by the Société Saint-Jean-Baptiste, this was one of the first multifunctional buildings in Canada. Today it belongs to the National Theatre School, and contains many different spaces capable of accommodating various shows. The National Monument and its refurbishment are justly considered an architectural achievement.

Théatre Saint-Denis

1594, rue Saint-Denis
M° Berri-UQAM
☎ (514) 849 4211
Prices vary depending on the show.

Completely renovated, Théâtre Saint-Denis welcomes above all comedy shows (it's the main venue for the Just For Laughs Montreal Festival) and big productions.

L

M

N

O

P

R

S

T

U

V

W

Published by AA Travel Publishing.

First published as Un grand week-end à Montréal: © Hachette Livre (Hachette Tourisme), 2005
Written by Sandrine Rabardeau
Maps within the book © Hachette Tourisme

Published by AA Publishing, a trading name of Automobile Association Developments Limited, whose registered office is Fanum House, Basing View, Basingstoke, Hampshire RG21 4EA. Registered number 1878835.

ISBN-10: 0-7495-4838-X
ISBN-13: 978-0-7495-4838-4

All rights reserved. No part of this publication may be reproduced, stored in a retrieval system, or transmitted in any form or by any means – electronic, photocopying, recording or otherwise – unless the written permission of the publishers has been obtained beforehand. This book may not be sold, resold, hired out or otherwise disposed of by way of trade in any form of binding or cover other than that in which it is published, without the prior consent of the publisher.

The contents of this publication are believed correct at the time of printing. Nevertheless, AA Publishing accept no responsibility for errors, omissions or changes in the details given, or for the consequences of readers' reliance on this information. This does not affect your statutory rights. Assessments of the attractions, hotels and restaurants are based upon the author's own experience and contain subjective opinions that may reflect the publisher's opinion or a reader's experience. We have tried to ensure accuracy, but things do change, so please let us know if you have any comments or corrections.

English translation © Automobile Association Developments Limited 2006
Translation work by G and W Advertising and Publishing

Cover design by Bookwork Creative Associates, Hampshire
Cover maps produced from map data © Tele Atlas N. V. 2003 and mapping © GEOnext (Gruppo De Agostini) Novara

Colour separation by Kingsclere Design and Print
Printed and bound in China by Leo Paper Products

Cover credits
Front cover : AA World Travel Library/J F Pin; **Back cover** : Nicolas Edwige

Picture credits
All the photographs are by **Nicolas Edwige**, with the exception of the following:

© Jardin botanique de Montréal : p. 16 (t.l.),
© Parc Jean-Drapeau, Sébastien Larose : p. 17 (t.c.),
© Tourisme Montréal, Stéphan Poulin : p. 20 (t.l.),
© Festival Montréal en Lumière, Jean-François Leblanc : p. 20 (t.r.),
© Festival International de Jazz de Montréal, Jean-François Leblanc : p. 20 (b.r.),
© Tourisme Montréal, Stéphan Poulin : p. 21 (t.r.),
© Festival International de Jazz de Montréal, Caroline Hayeur : p. 21 (b.r.),
© Parc Jean-Drapeau, Sébastien Larose : p. 23 (c.l.),
© Office national du Film du Canada, Jac-Mat : p. 27 (c.c.).

Illustrations

Virginia Pulm

A02680